Metamorphoses

For Maria X o H
ing
to
our Starstruck
conference

Elaine F.

OXFORD APPROACHES TO

CLASSICAL LITERATURE

SERIES EDITORS
Kathleen Coleman and Richard Rutherford

OVID'S *Metamorphoses*
ELAINE FANTHAM

PLATO'S *Symposium*
RICHARD HUNTER

OVID'S
Metamorphoses

ELAINE FANTHAM

OXFORD
UNIVERSITY PRESS

2004

OXFORD
UNIVERSITY PRESS

Oxford   New York
Auckland   Bangkok   Buenos Aires   Cape Town   Chennai
Dar es Salaam   Delhi   Hong Kong   Istanbul   Karachi   Kolkata
Kuala Lumpur   Madrid   Melbourne   Mexico City   Mumbai   Nairobi
São Paulo   Shanghai   Taipei   Tokyo   Toronto

Copyright © 2004 by Oxford University Press, Inc.

Published by Oxford University Press, Inc.
198 Madison Avenue, New York, New York 10016

www.oup.com

Oxford is a registered trademark of Oxford University Press

Library of Congress Cataloging-in-Publication Data
Fantham, Elaine.
Ovid's Metamorphoses / Elaine Fantham.
p.   cm. — (Oxford approaches to classical literature)
Includes bibliographical references and index.
ISBN 0-19-515409-6; 0-19-515410-X (pbk.)
1. Ovid, 43 B.C.–17 or 18 A.D. Metamorphoses   2. Fables,
Latin—History and criticism.   3. Mythology, Classical, in literature.
4. Metamorphosis in literature.   I. Title.   II. Series.
PA6519.M9 F36 2004
873'.01 —dc22   2003016164

1 3 5 7 9 8 6 4 2

Printed in the United States of America
on acid-free paper

Editors' Foreword

The late twentieth and early twenty-first centuries have seen a massive expansion in courses dealing with ancient civilization and, in particular, the culture and literature of the Greek and Roman world. Never has there been such a flood of good translations available: Oxford's own World Classics, the Penguin Classics, the Hackett Library, and other series offer the English-speaking reader access to the masterpieces of classical literature from Homer to Augustine. The reader may, however, need more guidance in the interpretation and understanding of these works than can usually be provided in the relatively short introduction that prefaces a work in translation. There is a need for studies of individual works that will provide a clear, lively, and reliable account based on the most up-to-date scholarship without dwelling on minutiae that are likely to distract or confuse the reader.

It is to meet this need that the present series has been devised. The title *Oxford Approaches to Classical Literature* deliberately puts the emphasis on the literary works themselves. The volumes in this series will each be concerned with a single work (with the exception of cases where a "book" or larger collection of poems is treated as one work). These are neither biographies nor accounts of literary movements or schools. Nor are they books devoted to the total oeuvre of one author: our first volumes consider Ovid's *Metamorphoses* and Plato's *Symposium*, not the works of Ovid or Plato as a whole. This is, however, a question of emphasis, and not a straitjacket: biographical issues, literary and cultural background, and related works by the same author are discussed where they are obviously relevant. The series' authors have also been encouraged to consider the influence and legacy of the works in question.

As the editors of this series, we intend these volumes to be accessible to the reader who is encountering the relevant work for the first time; but we also intend that each volume should do more than simply provide the basic facts, dates, and summaries that handbooks generally supply. We would like these books to be essays in criticism and interpretation that will do justice to the subtlety and complexity of the works under discussion. With this in mind, we have invited leading scholars to offer personal assessments and appreciation of their chosen work, anchored within the mainstream of classical scholarship. We have thought it particularly important that our authors be allowed to set their own agendas and speak in their own voices rather than repeating the *idées reçues* of conventional wisdom in neutral tones.

The title *Oxford Approaches to Classical Literature* has been chosen simply because the series is published by Oxford University Press, USA; it in no way implies a party line, either Oxonian or any other. We believe that different approaches are suited to different texts, and we expect each volume to have its own distinctive character. Advanced critical theory is neither compulsory nor excluded: what matters is whether it can be made to illuminate the text in question. The authors have been encouraged to avoid obscurity and jargon, bearing in mind the needs of the general reader; but, when important critical or narratological issues arise, they are presented to the reader as lucidly as possible.

This series was originally conceived by Professor Charles Segal, an inspiring scholar and teacher whose intellectual energy and range of interests were matched by a corresponding humility and generosity of spirit. Although he was involved in the commissioning of a number of volumes, he did not—alas—live to see any of them published. The series is intended to convey something of the excitement and pleasure to be derived from reading the extraordinarily rich and varied literature of Greco-Roman antiquity. We hope that these volumes will form a worthy monument to a dedicated classical scholar who was committed to enabling the ancient texts to speak to the widest possible audience in the contemporary world.

Kathleen Coleman, Harvard University
Richard Rutherford, Christ Church, Oxford

Preface

The *Metamorphoses* is too brilliant and marvelous (it is literally full of marvels) for anyone to do it justice in either a big book ("A big book is a big bore," as Callimachus said) or a small one. This short introductory study is supposed to serve as an appetizer, sending readers who do not yet have their own text to go and buy a version either in their own language or, better still, in Ovid's sparkling Latin. I have written it so that a reader can move through these chapters as he or she moves through Ovid's universal poetic history from creation to his own times. The main theme of chapter 1 is the "prehistory" of poems of transformation. Chapter 2 concerns *Metamorphoses,* books 1–2. Chapter 3 concentrates on Ovid's Theban cycle in books 3–4. Chapter 4 is devoted to artists in books 5 and 6, with an excursion forward into book 10. Only with chapters 5 (on women's lives) and 6 (on love, too short a fraction of both men's and women's lives) does the book move into the second half of the poem. From chapter 7 on we will be looking at all fifteen books, and chapter 10 will attempt to leap four tall buildings at a time with a scattered sampling of how Ovid's poem and its vernacular translations have influenced painting, poetry, fiction, and music over the last two millennia.

I deeply appreciated the compliment of being invited by Kathleen Coleman and the late Charles Segal to write this introduction. Charlie Segal, author of *Landscape in Ovid's Metamorphoses,* one of the most exciting books on the *Metamorphoses* to appear in the sixties, was also immensely kind in providing photocopies of many of his articles on Ovid. During and beyond my visits to Cambridge University, I have accumulated a great debt of gratitude to Ted Kenney and Philip Hardie for answering my questions and letting me see much of their work in advance of publication: I am more grateful than I may have been able to express. Indeed, since this is such a short book, there are far too many other scholars and critics whose ideas I have not been able to footnote. Let me thank here for the stimulus of their ideas Alessandro Barchiesi, Denis Feeney, Andrew Feldherr, Stephen Hinds, Alison Keith, John Miller, Sara Myers, Carole Newlands, Jim O'Hara, Gianpiero Rosati, Joe Solodow, Garth Tissol, and Stephen Wheeler, whose studies of the *Metamorphoses,* together with the work of Roy Gibson, Jim McKeown, and Katharina Volk on Ovidian elegy, have added so much to our understanding of Ovid in the last two decades. But others will recognize their ideas gathered like flowers in my mixed bouquet, and I can only ask their indulgence if they are not named and honored on this page. I have gratefully used A. D. Melville's elegant verse translation for many excerpts. Translations from *Metamorphoses* and other texts quoted without an acknowledgment are my own.

For their valuable guidance on my manuscript, I owe special thanks to Kathleen Coleman and her coeditor Richard Rutherford: both series editors have been models of patience and support, but Kathleen in particular has answered my every query and anticipated my difficulties. Any remaining lapses are, alas, entirely my own fault.

Contents

Ovid's
Metamorphoses

· 1 ·

Transforming Bodies,
Transforming Epic

Prologue

We cannot date exactly the publication—that is, the circulation in manuscript form—of Ovid's great epic of transformation. Our earliest report comes from the poet himself, but from a chastened Ovid, exiled to the northern edge of empire, to Tomis on the Romanian Black Sea coast, by the decree of Augustus. For almost thirty years Ovid had enjoyed popularity and fame as a poet of love, first with five books of poems in narrative or dramatic form illustrating his own love affairs (reduced to three books in a second edition), then with his *Letters from Heroines,* which presented, in character, the messages of Homeric and tragic heroines, even Virgil's Dido, to the husbands and lovers who had left them, then more elaborately with books of instruction in the art of love (two for men and one for girls—but not respectable women), and finally with a book of cures for love. There was an appetite in fashionable Rome for love affairs and poetry about such flirtations. But the women of the leader's family are expected to have higher standards. When first the daughter and then the granddaughter of First Citizen Augustus had been caught in flagrant adultery, Augustus exiled the poet, whether for his bad influence or for some more conspiratorial involvement with the princesses' circles.

Now, in 8 C.E., Ovid writes from Tomis about the fifteen volumes of his "Changing Forms," which he had let into the hands of readers, although they lacked the finishing touch. In a second reference he urges the owners of these volumes to insert six lines of explanation or excuse before his text:

> There are also the Changed Shapes, thrice five rolls of them, verses snatched from the funeral of their master. . . . so now accept these six verses as well, if you think them fit to be prefixed to the book's first sheet:
>
> "All you who touch these volumes orphaned of their poetic father, at least grant them a place in your city. To win your favor, they have not been made public by the poet himself, but, as it were, have been snatched from their master's pyre. Whatever faults this rough poem may have, he would have corrected, if he had been allowed to." (*Tristia* [Poems of Sadness] 1.7.12, 33–40)

But in a world where oral recitation normally preceded circulation in written form, Ovid must have read installments of his poem to chosen friends: a poem of such great length and complexity would have taken even the brilliant Ovid many years to compose. Why is his ambitious enterprise never mentioned until it is complete? And how would his friends have come to know the poem? We have to imagine that first recital for ourselves. Even the first four lines break with tradition and offer hidden challenges. Shall we listen?

In nova fert animus . . .
My fancy sweeps me to new themes . . .

(No: that's not what Ovid is saying.)

       mutatas dicere formas
Corpora . . .
       My fancy bids me sing of shapes transformed
into new bodies . . .

(But isn't it the other way round? Bodies are transformed into new shapes: it is the shapes that change.)

> *di, coeptis, nam vos mutastis et illa*
> *adspirate meis.*
>> Gods, inspire my task [or "work-in progress"]
> for you transformed that too.

In the second half of his second line Ovid springs a surprise—at least a surprise for his many enthusiastic fans, who were expecting the short end-stopped second line of the elegiac couplet. This isn't elegy after all. The second line is another regular epic hexameter. This really is something new from Ovid!

> *primaque ab origine mundi*
> *ad mea perpetuum deducite tempora carmen*
>> Spin out this song
> Unbroken from creation to my times.

Or as A. D. Melville translates in more seemly and harmonious verse:

Of bodies changed to other forms I tell;
You Gods, who have yourselves wrought every change,
Inspire my enterprise and lead my lay
In one continuous song from nature's first
Remote beginnings to our modern times.

How would Roman connoisseurs of poetry and poetic criticism react to this? Wouldn't they recall that Horace warned budding poets against beginning their epics too far back in time and narrating the Trojan War from the egg which hatched fair Helen? Isn't Ovid going over the top? And what sort of epic is this going to be: scientific didactic, like Lucretius's account of the universe, or mythological and legendary, like Virgil's *Aeneid,* or (gods forbid) a sort of updated Ennian celebration of imperial triumphs? Shouldn't he invoke the Great Leader's blessing, as Virgil did in his proem to the *Georgics?* Or at least Apollo or the Muses? Only when he has thoroughly bemused his readers (without help from any muse!) is Ovid ready to begin—at the beginning of it all.

Transforming Epic

So does Ovid makes his first foray in the meter of epic verse. But his narrative has no precedent. Traditional epic was unified by a single hero or people, whose fortunes it followed. It could be a simple versified chronicle of national history, which in turn could be defined by a historical event, like the *Punic War* of Naevius (though he seems to have included a retrospective narrative of the flight of Aeneas from Troy). Ennius, his successor, seems to have preferred an open-ended chronicle. His *Annals* originally followed national history from Romulus to the contemporary fighting against the Aetolians, but then Ennius extended their fifteen books to eighteen to include additional wars. Virgil had set Roman poets a new example for formal narrative. He modeled the early adventures of Aeneas on Homer's Odysseus and in some respects on Apollonius's saga of the Argonauts; the later books of his *Aeneid* were a counterpart to the *Iliad,* narrating the conflicts of Aeneas in Italy as he fulfilled his mission to ensure the foundation of Rome. Unified by its single hero, the epic was integrated by complex cross-reference and a climactic closure.

Another existing Roman model for narrative poetry was the miniature epic (often referred to as *epyllion*), which was constructed around a legendary romance and often incorporated another tale as a foil. This artful Hellenistic form had been adopted by Catullus for the wedding narrative of Peleus and Thetis, framing the abandonment and rescue of Ariadne. Two of his friends even used epic verse to tell stories of metamorphoses to which Ovid would return: in their poems, now lost, Calvus had composed the tale of Io's rape, transformation and wanderings, while Cinna had described Myrrha's illicit passion for her own father.

The Hellenistic poet and critic Callimachus offered another poetic model: the collecting of short, allusive, self-contained poems into a carefully arranged volume that played on internal balance and contrast. He proclaimed new critical standards, by which a poem should be highly refined, evoking more than it said, and he rejected the long narrative form as tedious. Callimachus had expressly praised the finespun and denounced the continuous unbroken poem. Here was Ovid declaring that he would write a long and totally comprehensive poem that was also finespun and refined. And the title implied that the poem would be a composite of many transformation tales. How could such a poem have an artistic form? It will be better to return to this and other aesthetic questions when we have become more familiar with the tales that Ovid told, and how he told them.

There are transformations in nature, from the obvious changes from egg to caterpillar to chrysalis to butterfly, to the more gradual changes in human growth and decay. But the transformations that made men wonder and stirred their fantasy were those that seemed contrary to nature, the marvels and miracles of folktale, myth, and legend. Greek literature, from Homer on, had shown a measure of restraint in its use of the motif of metamorphosis: there are, for instance, very few transformation tales in Homer, each of them distanced in some way from the world of his main narrative.

One occurs in the *Iliad*, where it is reported by Odysseus (not known for his love of truth) in his urgent appeal against abandoning the Greek siege of Troy. He recalls the time when the expedition was waiting to set out from Aulis, and the gods had sent a portent: a snake attacked and devoured a mother bird and her nine nestlings. But then, according to Odysseus, "the god Zeus, son of cunning Kronos, who had made the serpent appear, made him into a stone, and we all were amazed as we stood there" (*Il.* 2.318–21). Odysseus wants to remind the Greeks of Calchas's optimistic interpretation of the "great sign," and the serpent, like its victims, is removed from reality by its symbolic function.

This was the act of a god, to warn men and affect their future actions. So too the god Poseidon, with the authorization of Zeus, turns into stone the Phaeacian ship which has transported his enemy Odysseus safely to Ithaca (*Od.* 13.125–64). He has asked Zeus to punish the Phaeacians for disobeying his prohibition on carrying foreigners by destroying their ship in midvoyage and rearing up a mountain to isolate their city. Zeus permits him only to make the ship stone (there is no word for change, only for making) in full sight of the Phaeacians. Poseidon's purpose is so that "all men may marvel" (as in the *Iliad* portent), and so they do. Again the miracle is interpreted: by King Alcinoos, who recalls the prophecy and urges them to sacrifice to Poseidon before he destroys their city. But there are no miracles on Ithaca, where life is realistically portrayed. Although the Phaeacians live outside the world of Odysseus's fairy tale narratives of books 9–12, the way their city is introduced into the poem shows that nevertheless they are also beyond the normal Greek world of cities and islands.

These transformations are acts of the gods for human benefit and do not transform humans themselves (we hope that the Phaeacian ship is empty of its crew). But folktale reveled in wizards and witches, and Odysseus's tale of the witch Circe is our first example of humans victimized by a downward transformation, into animal form. It is a familiar story, but it is important to see how Homer tells it, because that will enable us to compare this early model of magical metamorphosis with the brilliant complex that Ovid makes of Circe and her magic powers. When Odysseus lands with his comrades on her island, they see the smoke arising from her hearth and Odysseus sends Eurylochus with half the men to reconnoiter. Homer himself reports that the apparently tame wolves and lions around Circe's palace had been bewitched by Circe with evil drugs. She welcomes the men with a drink containing a drug to make them forget their homes and country, and when they have drunk it, she strikes them with her wand, so that they take on the voice, heads, bristles, and bodies of swine, but their minds are unchanged.

It has been suggested by some critics that the drugs do not cause the metamorphosis but merely change the drinkers' state of mind, like Helen's Nepenthe, the drink of forgetfulness. But why should we doubt Eurylochus, the only man who does not drink but who escapes to tell Odysseus what has happened? This is direct narrative, confirmed by the god Hermes, who meets Odysseus and arms him with an antidote (the herb Moly) and instructions; after eating this he will not be affected by Circe's potion, but he must draw his sword on her and make her swear an oath not to harm him. Odysseus is successful and, after enjoying her hospitality, forces Circe to release his men. They come from the sty looking like nine-year-old pigs, but when she smears them with another drug (the poet is not specific!), they lose their bristles and become men again, "younger than they were before, and more handsome, and larger to look upon." The rejuvenation is a very pleasant touch.

Does this metamorphosis have a reason, a motive? Homer does not make this a moral tale about the consequences of gluttony—as he does when the sailors steal the cattle of the sun. Tales of magic are by their nature apart from the morality of reward and punishment. This is simply an ancient horror story, and Circe's only motive seems to be a demonstration of her power, though it could be read as self-protection from violation by invaders. Because these tales of magic seem so arbitrary they form only a small proportion of the many ancient legends of metamorphosis, but Circe, like her cousin Medea, would continue to dominate the imagination of mythmakers and poets.

Ovid's great predecessor Virgil was more cautious: when he took Aeneas on his voyage to Sicily, the hero was warned to avoid the terrible hazards suffered by Odysseus: the sea monsters Scylla and Charybdis and the shores of the Cyclops. Using local legend, Virgil placed Circe on the island (really a promontory) of Monte Circeii, south of Rome, so that Aeneas does not pass it until he is on the last lap of his voyage, coming from Cumae to the Tiber mouth. Virgil describes evocatively the remote glades of Circe and the odor of sweet cedar from her oil lamps as she weaves by night. There is the charming sound of her singing at her task, but set against it are the angry growls of lions protesting their chains and of bristly swine, bears, and "the shapes of great wolves" (not wolves, but their outward shape) whom the goddess had cruelly transformed from the appearance of men into the features and bodies of wild animals" (*Aen.* 7.10–20). But Aeneas is not put at risk: when his fleet approaches by night, Neptune sends winds to keep them on course so that the Trojans escape such unnatural experiences (*monstra*).

Ovid goes to the other extreme: he will give his readers not only the full *Odyssey* narrative in the eyewitness account of Odysseus's (hitherto unknown) comrade Macareus but also a preliminary piece of sorcery—Circe's metamorphosis of Scylla into the sea monster—and a tailpiece set nearer to Rome. Circe becomes the link in a moving chain of love stories that carries his narrative from Sicily to Latium. First Glaucus, newly become a sea god, goes to Circe for help when his beloved Scylla rejects him. Circe's palace is described as "full of assorted wild beasts," and Glaucus greets this child of the Sun as "Goddess" (*Met.* 14.10–12). Ovid's Circe, however, is a nymphomaniac and offers herself to her guest. When he rejects her, she decides to victimize her rival, Scylla, and brews evil plants with dread juices, activating them with the spells of Hecate (Roman magic seems to require spells, which Homer omits). Passing through the fawning animal captives she walks dry-shod over the waves to Scylla's favorite pool, pours her poison into it, and bewitches it with a spell repeated nine times thrice. Poor Scylla is afflicted with a monstrous form, her loins sprouting dogs, as soon as she enters the water (14.60–7). This is the monster who will rob Odysseus/Ulysses of his men, but Ovid adds slyly that Scylla will undergo a further transformation into a rock before there is any risk of her attacking the Trojan ships.

Our poet is playing more than one game—with witchcraft, which he will exaggerate beyond tradition (Circe never walked the waters), and with the epic poets who went before him. Thus, he includes the original Homeric episode in the narrative of Macareus, his invented companion of Ulysses. As Eurylochus told Ulysses, so Macareus tells his old companion and Ovid's readers how he went with Eurylochus in the group whom Circe bewitched (14.245–307). The tale is enriched with colorful detail, as the men are greeted by Circe's menagerie and find her in a golden robe, seated on her throne, not weaving (Ovid is quite clear about "correcting" Virgil) but supervising the herb gathering of her nymphs and instructing them. She orders up the Homeric brew of barley, honey, milk, and wine, adding her drug, and as soon as they have drained it (and been tapped on the head) Macareus feels the bristles sprout, loses his voice in grunting, falls to the ground, and feels his snout growing and his hands turning to hooves. They are penned in the sty— and if Eurylochus had not refused and fled, they would still be penned there. Rapidly Ovid sketches in Ulysses' rescue mission and conquest of Circe. As dowry (!) for their mating he demands the release of the comrades, and the process goes into reverse. Starting true to Homer, Macareus has them sprinkled with the "the better juices of an unknown herb" and tapped on the head with Circe's wand—now inverted—as she utters words opposite to her former words (14.299–301; but there were no spells in Homer). What Ovid most enjoys is the inverse transformation:

> The more she sang her charms, the more erect
> We rose; our bristles fell; our cloven feet
> Forsook their clefts; our shoulders, elbows, arms,
> Came back again. (14.302–5)

Ingeniously Ovid retells and makes new and fresh the oldest human transformation known to us. But although he relishes the moments of transformation, he also relishes the personalities, and his nymphomaniac Circe is the protagonist of another human transformation, briefly mentioned by Virgil. Virgil describes the statue of a legendary Latin prince, called Picus (woodpecker), portrayed as an armed warrior in the palace of his descendant Latinus, and alludes to Circe as "his lustful wife, who had turned him into a bird striking him with her gold wand and transforming him with poison" (*Aen.* 7.187–91).

In Macareus's narrative the maid he befriends shows him a strange statue of a youth with a woodpecker on his head. The statue stands in a shrine and is honored with garlands as a cult object. And this, says Macareus, is the tale she told. Now it is the maid who explains about the love of the prince Picus for the nymph Canens; how Circe goes gathering herbs and comes upon Picus as he is boar hunting and takes a fancy to him. Using her magic powers Circe creates a phantom boar to lead him astray and prays to unknown gods (a common feature of magic in Ovid's own time) with her regular formula to make the moon or sun eclipse (14.358–68). Thus, she is able to darken the sky and calls up mists which separate Picus from his escort. But when she accosts him, openly praising his beauty of form (which she will destroy to punish him) and proudly introduces herself by her name and divine parentage, she meets another rejection, as he courteously explains he is another woman's beloved. The pattern of the Glaucus episode is repeated, but this time it is the man she punishes. Turning twice to west and twice to east, she touches him three times with her wand, uttering three spells. Although he tries desperately to escape, he realizes that he is becoming a bird, and he attacks the trees in anger. The prince's crimson cloak becomes the bird's red back; and his golden brooch, a ring of golden feathers around his neck (14.386–96). It is not Circe's powers but grief for her lost love that makes the faithful Canens pine away, singing lament until she melts into thin air.

Thus, Ovid has multiplied Circe's power, lavishing details of her magic ritual and supernatural control of human perceptions and natural phenomena on the bare acts of transformation. He uses the ruthless witch to demonstrate to his readers what Circe threatens her victims with: just what a wronged and loving woman can do— that is, if she is Circe (14.384–5). How could the maid have known all this, including Picus's emotions, and why is Circe honoring his statue? Like a modern mystery writer Ovid moves quickly away from the mystery and back through Macareus to Aeneas and his next landfall. This brilliant storytelling has drawn on motifs from a tradition that had grown increasingly rich since the narrative of the *Odyssey*.

Homer's Olympians could metamorphose themselves, and several gods take the form of specific human beings or types of person in both the *Iliad* and the *Odyssey*. But they do not take animal form, as Zeus did in so many seduction stories of later Greek art and poetry, most familiar to us in the versions told by Ovid. He did not invent the tales of Zeus seducing Europa as a bull or Danae as a shower of gold or Leda as a swan: he even quotes them as proof of the untrustworthiness of poets (*Amores* 3.12). And it was poets, Ovid declares, who invented Proteus, the archetypal self-transformer, who could change his own shape as a defense mechanism. Proteus is the supernatural old man of the sea who features in the traveler's tale told by Menelaus to Odysseus's son Telemachus in *Odyssey* 4: how the goddess Eidothea helped him to discover how to get favorable winds when he was in Egypt. She explains that her father, Proteus, knows everything but will not give away his supernatural knowledge unless he is physically compelled. Menelaus must go to the offshore island of Pharos and lie in wait when Proteus comes from the sea at noon to rest. The old man will go through a series of transformations, becoming all the creatures on earth and then sea and fire, but Menelaus must hold on grimly, until Proteus is exhausted and returns to his own human shape and speech; then he can ask Proteus what he will (*Od.* 4.400–424). Menelaus obeys, and Proteus becomes a lion, a serpent, a leopard, and a boar, then water and even a tall, branching tree but finally answers all his questions, advising him and telling him the fate of his brother and friends. This mythical shape-shifter has sometimes been explained in terms of squids; certainly he and other beings with this power have watery ancestry and associations.

Virgil was the first Roman poet to adapt this tale, with some changes (it is not Proteus's daughter, as in the *Odyssey,* who betrays his secret); in fact, Virgil is the first poet to use the verb "transform": Proteus "transforms himself into every kind of marvelous being." The vividness of Virgil's narrative (*Georgics* 4.387–529) explains why Ovid, who knew the story well and alludes to it in his other poetry, chose not to rewrite it in his *Metamorphoses.* But he does introduce shape-shifters halfway through his great chain of stories, on the lips of a self-described shape-shifter, the river Achelous. There are, says Achelous, "transformable bodies," and as a prelude to telling about his own defeat by Hercules, he introduces the tale of the girl Mnestra, who was constantly sold by her penniless father but escaped each master by changing into another human shape—whether male or female. Later Ovid introduces two more shape-shifters: the sea-maiden Thetis, who used her skills to evade rape but was overcome by Peleus (whom Proteus had briefed on how to approach her), and the Italian god of disguise, Vertumnus ("the Turner," from Latin *vertere*), who used the same skills to become an old woman go-between and commend himself to the chaste Pomona.

Metamorphosis might seem quite alien to the stage, and certainly few Greek tragedies report them, but the author of *Prometheus Bound* brings Io as a horned maiden to converse with Prometheus and explain how she was, not transformed, but expelled from her family. Euripides too gives to "gods from the machine" two prophecies of metamorphosis which Ovid will include in his poem: that of Cadmus and Harmonia into serpents, and of Hecuba into a snarling bitch. But it was the lesser myths of minor nymphs and heroes that attracted the antiquarian curiosity of the Hellenistic cataloguers and poets. Indeed, the same man might record a catalogue of metamorphoses in prose and compose a poem around one or more such tales. Nicander wrote the five poetry books of *Heteroeoumena* (Beings made alien), which partly survive in a compendium written by Antoninus Liberalis more than a century after Ovid; in fact, Ovid uses more than a third of the myths reported from Nicander. A mysterious Boios (who may have been a woman, Boio) wrote *Ornithogonia* (The origins of birds), which Ovid seems to know, and a generation before Ovid the poet Cinna triumphantly brought to Rome the Greek scholar-poet Parthenius, who wrote a poem of metamorphoses, now lost, and a surviving collection of tales of passion excerpted from earlier writers, some of which include transformations. Parthenius, who taught Virgil, compiled them as raw material for his patron, the poet Gallus, to turn into elegiac or epic verse. And Virgil himself may have planned to write poetry about these metamorphoses: certainly he includes five such transformations as themes of Silenus's song in his sixth *Eclogue*.

But readers would soon be bored if the poet gave them only arbitrary narratives of transformation. Instead, Ovid, like the Greeks before him, interpreted many of the old myths as divine acts of justice or mercy: a god or gods would reward just and pious people with a desired transformation, as the good fairy would make Cinderella appear to be a beautiful princess and win the prince and would punish the wicked sisters with deformities. And the same myth could be reinterpreted with a different slant, just as the Middle Ages would find a way to make Ovid acceptable by imposing a Christian moral in *Ovide moralisé*. One of Ovid's most tender love stories is the transformation of Alcyone and her drowned husband, Ceyx, into the halcyon birds who nest on the sea in a special period of winter calm; but an earlier Greek version of their fate had them turned into birds to punish them for boastfully calling themselves Zeus and Hera. Mercy is often shown when a god "takes pity" on a virgin pursued by a rapist or on a bereaved wife or mother who is pining away with grief and saves them by removing human form. Most traditional tales of metamorphosis dealt with humans changed downward, into lower forms of life—animals or plants—or even into inanimate rocks and water. Yet for centuries before Ovid there had been tales about men or women transformed into stars as a kind of deification, as Bacchus had deified Ariadne, or changed into immortal demigods and nymphs. A very few were even raised to heaven, to join the Olympians, as Heracles and Castor and Pollux, heroes with divine fathers, were reputed to have become gods. The Romans had their own myths of deification, adding Aeneas and Romulus by analogy with the Greek heroes, and would take over from the posthumous cult of Alexander the Great the cult practice of deifying their greatest and most powerful leaders at their death. But here we touch on a very complex political issue: Ovid's handling of the deified Julius Caesar as he approaches the end of his great poem will show just how tricky it could be to deal with such controversial ideas when the ideology of the ruling power was offensive to many in the former ruling class.

The *Metamorphoses* would never have won centuries of readers if Ovid had not known how to appeal to both the head and the heart, to imagination as well as sentiment, to our feeling for the tragic and our amusement at the comic, to our response to visual arts and to human vulnerability. Again, transformations alone could not provide a satisfying story, if only because metamorphosis is a kind of death, which normally brings a narrative to an abrupt end. Instead, Ovid engages us emotionally in a personal situation and, by focalizing his narrative through the victim of transformation, commits us to sharing his or her feelings. Let me illustrate from the narrative of Io, which occupies the second half of his first book. An earlier Roman poet, Calvus, had constructed a miniature epic around her transformation, and a snatch of this lost poem commiserates with Io on enduring the diet of a cow: "Ah, unhappy maiden, you will feed on bitter grasses!"

Ovid is more oblique. We slide into the story when her father, Inachus, is missing from a gathering of river gods in the Thessalian palace of Peneus. His daughter has disappeared, and he does not know whether she is alive or in the underworld (as, for instance, Proserpina was kidnapped to the underworld by Dis). In a flashback Ovid reports how Jupiter spied Io. He describes Jupiter's technique of addressing her with flattery and inviting her to shelter from the sun in the woods; she will have a god to protect her—and no common or garden god, but Jupiter, who rules the world and wields the thunder. When she tries to escape, he envelops her in darkness and possesses her (1.588–600). But this is not just rape, it is adultery, and Juno spots the mysterious cloud and suspects the worst. It is to conceal his guilt that Jupiter now changes Io's appearance—in one line—into a snow-white cow, which his wife now requests of him as a present. Ovid shares with us Jupiter's dilemma: he does not want to lose his beloved, but to refuse will show that she is not just a cow.

Juno in turn is not reassured and puts the multi-eyed Argos on Io's tail. He herds her everywhere and tethers her at night, feeding her on bitter herbs (the same diet that had distressed Calvus) and muddy streams. When she tries to plead with Argos, her words become moos and she cannot raise her arms in supplication. Now comes the moment of real pathos as Io returns home to graze and sees her horns in the waters of her father's river. Seeing one's own animal form has to be the worst moment for the metamorphosed, as it was for Kafka's Joseph K. when he realizes that he has become a giant cockroach. Virgil's Silenus imagines the fears of the daughters of Proetus, whose bodies were unchanged but who were deluded into believing they were cows: "they filled the fields with imaginary lowing, but none of them sought shameful intercourse with cattle, though each feared the plow-yoke on her neck and often searched for horns on her smooth brow" (*Eclogue* 6.48–51).

Io catches sight of her father and follows him, licking his hands: "If only words would come / She'd speak her name," but since she cannot speak, she scrawls her name, Io, with her hoof as the sad sign of her transformed body (*corporis . . . mutati*). Ovid has set this story in a world of domestic comedy, adulterous husbands, and innocent daughters made pregnant. So when her father understands her fate, he bewails the loss of a good marriage alliance: now, instead of a human bridegroom, he will have to find her a mate from the herd; worse, being immortal, he will not be able to end his grief in death. Argos cuts short the lament and moves her on, but Jupiter has thought of a countermeasure and, like a comic lover, sends Mercury to trick her guardian into a fatal sleep.

At this point, the reader, who knows the legend, may slacken attention, so the poet slyly has Mercury (in disguise as a shepherd) distract Argos with an elaborate account of Pan's attempted rape of Syrinx. When Argos falls asleep just as the rapist is approaching his victim (1.700), Ovid himself takes over the narrative and polishes it off for the reader in twelve lines. Mercury neatly cuts Argos's throat, and the poet pauses just long enough to utter a two-line epigram to the deceased monster and explain how Juno took his eyes to decorate the tail of her peacock. It is also typical of Ovid's skill in varying his pace that after devoting a hundred and fifty lines to Io's rape and failed homecoming, he will accelerate to summarize in ten lines (1.724–34) how Juno sends a Fury to persecute the cow-maiden and drive her as a refugee across the world, until she comes to Egypt. There by the river Nile (she is, after all, a river god's daughter) Io kneels at the water's edge to raise her eyes—the only part of her body she can raise to the sky—in appeal to Jupiter. He in turn now appeases his wife and swears a mighty oath that Io will never cause her trouble again. As Juno relents, Io resumes her human shape, in one of the very few reverse transformations to occur in mythical tradition (Ulysses' companions are the only other instance I can recall):

> Io regained
> Her shape, became once more what once she was.
> The hair falls from her hide, her horns are gone,
> Her great wide eyes contract, her gaping mouth
> Shrinks small again, her arms and hands return,
> Her cloven hoofs resume their fivefold form;
> The heifer vanished, save her fair white grace.
> The nymph, content to use two legs again,
> Now walked erect, yet still afraid to speak,
> Lest, cow-like, she might moo, and timorously
> Essayed the syllables so long disused. (1.738–46,
> tr. Melville)

It is another important feature of Ovidian narrative that he puts so much stress on speech as the mark of humanity. Whenever a person is transformed into a lower form of life, the poet will emphasize this loss of speech and of power to communicate with other humans.

The tone of the Io story has combined genuine pathos with comedy, beginning as it does with her family and involving Jupiter as an erring husband. It will end by carrying the family on to the next generation and transforming itself into a boys' quarrel between Io's divine child, Epaphus, and Phaethon, child of Clymene and the sun god (a connection entirely invented by Ovid), to lead into his cautionary tale of Phaethon's fatal chariot ride. Because so many old myths are set outside chronology, the poet is free to select and arrange them as he chooses and to create his own ingenious transitions.

I quoted in full Ovid's piecemeal restoration of Io's form, and the four lines that reflect her mental condition. He will focus more often on the psychological impact of metamorphosis than on its physical process, but there are other episodes with less emotional content in which the poet delights in itemizing the transformation by body part. Thus, when the scoffer Acmon taunts Venus, "his voice, his throat grew thin, his hair became / Feathers, and feathers clothed his new-formed neck / And breasts and back, and larger plumage spread / Over his arms. His elbows made a curve / Of buoyant wings, webbed feet replaced his toes, / Hard horn his mouth—it finished in a beak" (14.498–503, tr. Melville). Fifty lines beyond comes Ovid's only upward transformation from inanimate to human (well, semidivine) form: the metamorphosis of Aeneas's ships into sea nymphs. Virgil had invented this miracle of the mother goddess, who intervened to save the burning ships that had been built from her sacred wood. He took some criticism for his narrative, although he avoided the embarrassment of physical specificity by making the ships plunge under the waves like dolphins, to reemerge as nymphs. It is likely that Ovid had heard just this kind of criticism, but he rose to the challenge with a particularly bold tour de force of part-by-part transformation. As the Mother goddess submerges the ships,

> Timber softened, and the wood
> Was changed to flesh, the curved prows turned to heads,
> The oars to toes and swimming legs, the sides
> Remained as sides; the keels that underlay
> The centre of the ship became a spine,
> The rigging soft sleek hair, the yards were arms,
> The colour sea-blue still, and in the waves
> They used to fear, they play their girlish games.
>   (14.549–57, tr. Melville)

After the anatomical changes, the poet again takes modern readers by surprise. We do not expect nymphs to be sea-blue, but in the Latin imagination the same word, *caeruleus,* conveyed both the shifting hues of the sea and the supposed complexion of sea gods and nymphs. On the other hand, modern readers may be more inclined than the ancient reader to think of ships as feminine personalities, and so less surprised when Ovid goes on to talk of his naval nymphs as having human loyalties. They gladly gave help to sailors but—here Ovid carries us back to his Homeric archetype—gloated over Odysseus's shipwreck and the moment when the timbers of the Phaeacian ship were engulfed in stone.

But before he introduces us to any tales of men and gods, Ovid has to create his universe: our next chapter will consider his cosmogony and the successive ordeals of the natural world by flood and fire.

Further Reading

For a general introduction to Ovid, see E. J. Kenney, in *Cambridge History of Classical Literature*, ed. E. J. Kenney and W. V. Clausen (Cambridge, 1982), 420–57. There is a fine short appreciation of the *Metamorphoses* by Kenney in *Ovid, "Metamorphoses,"* tr. A. D. Melville (Oxford 1986). Among book-length studies, note G. Karl Galinsky, *Ovid's "Metamorphoses": An Introduction to the Basic Aspects* (Berkeley, 1975); Joseph B. Solodow, *The World of Ovid's "Metamorphoses"* (Chapel Hill, 1988); Stephen M. Wheeler, *A Discourse of Wonders* (Philadelphia, 1999). On the figure of Circe, see C. P. Segal, "Circean Temptations," *Transactions of the American Philological Association* 99 (1968): 419–42. On transformations in Greek literature, see P. M. C. Forbes Irving, *Metamorphosis in Greek Myths* (Oxford, 1990).

·2·

Creation, Flood, and Fire

Creating Cosmos from Chaos

How does one kick-start a cosmogony? And what models did Ovid have for his representation of the beginning of the universe? Roman thought depended on Greek, and the Greek natural philosophers seem to have had three models for their conception of the birth of the cosmos: some represented it as a living organism, others as an artifact created by a divine being, and yet others in terms of a political or social entity. In fact, Plato combines the first and second models in the *Timaeus,* with "a god who took over all that was visible: seeing that it was not in a state of rest but in a state of discordant and disorderly motion, he brought it into order out of disorder" (*Tim.* 30a). "To make things good he constructed reason within soul and soul within body [i.e., matter] as he constructed the universe. . . . this cosmos has truly come into existence as a living creature endowed with soul and reason owing to the providence of the god" (*Tim.* 30b). The universe was a product of design, and for most Greek thinkers it was anthropocentric, designed for man's benefit, as the system of heavenly bodies itself was geocentric, constructed around the earth and not the sun.

The poets conceived of nothing so complex. For both Homer and Hesiod, the cosmos consisted of earth, sky and sea, with the heavenly bodies (the sun, moon, and stars), but for Hesiod at least there had to be a prior stage of chaos before the stable earth could emerge. And chaos was not so much void as a primordial soup. The major point of dissension arose between the Platonic tradition, which was continued by Aristotle and the Stoics, and Plato's near-contemporaries, the atomists Leucippus and Democritus. Democritus argued that the cosmos was neither unique nor immortal but was one of many possible and destructible worlds, being the product not of design but of the mechanical interaction of the atoms within the void. This picture of the "nature of the world" was developed by Epicurus and was expounded at Rome by the poet Lucretius, some fifty years before Ovid. It is this atomistic cosmogony which Virgil celebrates in the song of Silenus:

> Seeds of earth and wind and sea gathered in the great void with those of liquid fire. Now all elements came from these beginnings and the young sphere of the world formed: then the ground hardened and began to cut off Nereus in the sea and to take on the shapes of things. Already the earth was amazed at the new sun dawning and the rains fell from on high as clouds were dispelled and the woods first began to grow and the few living creatures wandered through unfamiliar hills. (*Eclogue* 6.31–40)

I have quoted this in full because Ovid knew it well, but he takes a different approach. He also knew the poetry of Lucretius and, before him, of Homer and Hesiod and was familiar with the beliefs of both the Epicurean and the Stoic philosophical schools. What he seems to have done is to devise a version that would touch on as many forms of tradition as possible. Thus, he opens with the Homeric triad of sea, earth, and sky and then casts back to the original chaos, combining the idea of Hesiodic void with Lucretian space— and in it a raw mass or heap of conflicting seeds of things. There was not yet any sun or moon, nor was the earth poised in the surrounding air with the ocean reaching around it. Everything was fluctuating, with no constant form (a reminder of Ovid's own theme of changing forms), so that the earth offered no firm standing, nor the water swimming; the sky was without light, and in the single undifferentiated body of matter, opposites clashed, cold with hot, dry with wet, soft with hard, and weightless with weighty elements.

This is Ovid's universe, an unsettled stew of atoms, until a god (or a superior or kinder Nature) intervenes and resolves the quarrel. This god separated off earth from sky, and water from earth, and the clear heaven from the thick atmosphere. (Now the tripartite world has resolved itself into the four elements of Empedocles and the Stoics: earth, sea, and two layers above, the crude air in which winds and weather rampage and the pure fiery ether beyond.) Ovid describes how, once the god had separated them into different spaces, he bound them up by a harmonious peace agreement. In this language of arbitration between the quarreling elements we meet the political model of cosmogony mentioned above, as if the anarchic universe was some multiple territorial dispute which only a god could settle.

Now the poet imagines layers generated by weight and weightlessness, as "the fiery force of the vaulted and weightless sky shoots upward, claiming its place at the summit; air comes next to it in lightness and position, while earth, being thicker, attracted the large elements and was burdened by its own weight; last of all, water occupied the lowest layer and enclosed the solid sphere" (1.26–31). Once this unidentified god has arranged and divided the mass, he can proceed to make the earth habitable. Why does he now roll the earth into the shape of a great ball? The poet's explanation—to ensure it was even in all directions—is a rather strange one, to which we shall return. Next he spreads the seas around, bidding them surge with the winds—another oddity, as we shall see—and surround the shores of the land. But sea is only part of water. Now the creator adds freshwater springs, pools, and lakes and encloses the rivers with banks; the rivers will be absorbed into the land or join the sea and beat on the shores instead of their banks. He makes the plains stretch out, the valleys sink, and forests rise on the stony mountains. The Hellenistic geographer Eratosthenes had understood and described the climates of the polar, tropical, and equatorial regions, and Ovid follows him (and Virgil) in seeing the world as divided into five climatic zones, of which the equatorial was too hot to live in, while the polar regions were buried in snow. Only the two zones enclosing the Tropics enjoyed a proper blend of heat and cool.

Over earth and sea hovers the air, and Ovid adds, echoing Plato, that there is the same proportion of weight between each of the four elements: in Ovid's words, "air is as much heavier than fire as earth is lighter than water." But his focus is now on the lower atmosphere, as he describes the phenomena this god ordains for it: mists and rains and thunder and "winds which make the lightning flashes." Yet his readers are reassured that the creator controls the places occupied by the winds, brothers so quarrelsome that they almost tear the world apart. Thinking now in terms of contemporary lands and peoples, Ovid describes the origins of each wind in the four quarters of the earth (1.56–66). Over the three elements of earth, sea, and air, and their contents, the god sets the clear and weightless ether, free of all pollution. This is in fact an elegant reprise of the earlier ordering of the four elements by weight and introduces the next stage: now that the maker of the universe has demarcated each layer, Ovid populates them. The stars leap out of darkness to twinkle all over the sky, sharing it with the "forms of the gods," the waters are allotted to the fish, earth takes on the wild beasts, and air, now fit to fly in, receives the birds.

There are a number of anomalies in this account, most of them springing from the poet's assumption that the universe was made for man. In its raw state, it is not fit for him to walk on land or swim in the sea, but Ovid does not call the sky unfit to fly in—since man cannot fly; instead, he points to its lack of light (which man will need) and saves the idea of "flyability" for the birds. His god makes the seas swell with the winds before he has created winds, and Ovid stresses the comfortable temperature of the zones around the Tropics before he has introduced man to benefit from it. (Virgil had made the same point, but after man was part of his world; however, Ovid is working his way toward man.) By the time Ovid reaches thunder and lightning, he is explicit about their power to terrify mankind (1.55), and two lines later he recalls present-day struggles with storm winds and describes the points of the compass in terms of human communities like the kingdom of Nabataean Arabia. It is all deliberate, of course. In just the same way, when he talks of "the forms of the gods" occupying heaven, the phrase both recalls his theme and evokes the constellations named after the figures their stars supposedly outlined. (His own first constellation will be Callisto, the Great Bear.)

After the birds, beasts, and fishes, there is only one kind of creature left, mankind, a more high-minded creature able to control all the others. Let there be man! He was needed, so now he is created, in three bare words (*natus homo est,* 1.78). But the poet is undecided whether this being was made by the creator god from divine seed, or whether earth still kept some residual seeds of heaven, which Prometheus mixed with rainwater to mold into the likeness of the gods. He seems to favor the latter explanation, but his language allows for a change of subject in midsentence so that not Prometheus but the creator god enabled man to stand erect and gave him a face that could look upward at the sky. This at least is Ovid's version of how "the earth once raw and shapeless changed to put on the previously unknown likeness of men" (1.87–88).

A number of phrases in this outline reinforce the image of the creator as a craftsman. I have translated *rudis* as raw, in the sense of rough, unworked material: before the craftsman god works on it, matter is *iners,* that is, without art. The divine artisan rolls the earth like a ball of clay to make it even, because that is what a potter or maker of statuettes would do; and it is as a statuette-maker that Prometheus, son of Iapetus, molded (*finxit*) man from clay and water in the image (*effigiem*) of the gods, and the earth put on the molded shapes (*figurae*) of men. The tale is a blend of Protagoras's myth in which Prometheus worked on human and animal creation and Callimachus's mockery of humans as "shapes molded from mud." The *Metamorphoses* will repeatedly appeal to the standards of art and celebrate artistry for its ability to compete with and outdo nature, not least when the sculptor Pygmalion shapes his ideal maiden of ivory and the goddess of love breathes life into his creation (see ch. 4).

But there may be another model behind Ovid's set-piece creation of the world. In the *Iliad* Homer had given to the craftsman god Hephaestus the task of making a divine shield for Achilles, and Virgil showed Vulcan crafting a similar shield for Aeneas. Each shield contained a number of complex images reflecting many aspects of the world, but in particular the description of Achilles' shield began with the god depicting earth and sky and sea, and ended with the border of Ocean that was set around the scenes on land. It has been suggested that Ovid deliberately evoked the round shield of Achilles by his opening line 5 and the reference to the edges of the earth in lines 13–14: "nor had Amphitrite stretched her arms around the long edge of earth." Certainly, the way in which the god successively produces each element at lines 36–7, 43, 55, and 67 recalls the way Virgil's Vulcan adds each new element of his composite; again, Ovid's description is obsessively spatial and symmetrical, displacing the organization of creation in successive time by the various arrangements of zones and atmosphere around a spatial center.

Were Ovid's listeners or his readers supposed to recognize all these elements in his neat and complex narrative? It is likely, I think, that they would approach it as the latest version of a favorite theme and expect to hear both some echoes of current philosophical systems and reminders of the epic and didactic tradition. If they did not, they would still emerge with a sense that this particular cosmogony made an artist out of the creator, and a wonderful interacting adult toy out of his creation.

How Mankind Earned Destruction

Besides Hesiod's narrative of divine creation in the *Theogony*, he also shaped in his *Works and Days* an influential myth of the successive ages of man. It is this myth that Ovid adapts to portray the four successive ages of metal: degenerating from the golden race (it is the men, not their setting, who bear the name golden age or generation) through the silver and bronze to the brutish age of iron (1.89–150). Hesiod indeed believed he was living in the age of iron; but Ovid makes the transition from his age of gold coincide with the divine succession from Saturn (Kronos) and assigns to the rule of his son Jupiter the second age, of silver. For Ovid, the members of the golden race are both innocent and happy, though he does not determine whether their happy life springs from innocence or from physical circumstances. They need no laws to keep them pious, no penalties or courts; they have no ships for trading, no weapons for war, and no farming or mining, because they live on wild foods such as fruit and acorns. It is a time of unending spring, producing flowers and grain without effort, and rivers run with milk and nectar, while honey drips from trees.

Jupiter reduced this springtime to a mere season between the harsh heat of summer and the icy chill of winter, driving men to make houses for shelter and sow seeds, making oxen groan beneath the plow. The age of bronze succeeded the age of silver and, although more violent, was not yet wicked; this comes only with the fourth age, that of iron, when greed brought treachery. Men trespassed on the sea for profit and staked claims on the earth, which had until then been common property; they even raped the earth for precious metals and developed war, banditry, and bloodshed. This age violated the bonds of hospitality and kinship, trampling on piety until the spirit of justice abandoned an earth saturated with blood. Into this dramatic decline Ovid feeds an alternative account based on Hesiod's *Theogony*, from which, however, he seems to distance himself by prefacing it with "men say." "Men say" that the giants born of earth and sky attacked the new Olympians, and when Jupiter struck them with his thunderbolt, he crushed them on the ground. Earth, soaked with their blood, created a new race of men who showed their origin in blood by their savage and bloodthirsty natures.

Whether iron age men were descended from ancestors in the earlier ages or were a new generation sprung from giants' blood, they were evil, and Ovid returns his narrative to the divine perspective. Jupiter groans with a godlike wrath, recalling the recent offense against him by King Lycaon, and summons a divine council. Such divine councils occurred in the *Iliad* and *Odyssey,* and Virgil had provided a fine example of Jupiter's divine impartiality between the quarreling goddesses in the council of *Aeneid* 10. Ovid's Jupiter, though, is far from impartial, and our reading of his behavior is complicated by the poet's ambiguous analogies between the loyal and obedient divine council and the nobles of the Roman senate, and between Lycaon's outrageous offenses against Jupiter and an evil conspiracy against the blood of the Caesars. If Jupiter is Augustus, he does not reflect credit upon him. He opens the meeting with the verdict that mankind must be destroyed, before their corruption spreads to the rest of creation, such as the harmless demigods, nymphs, and satyrs. "What hope is there of protecting these lesser creatures when Lycaon has conspired against *me,* the thunderer and ruler of you all?" But after their protests of loyal indignation, Jupiter reveals that he has already punished Lycaon for violating the obligations of hospitality by offering his guest a meal of human flesh. He has hurled his bolt against Lycaon's palace and sent him howling into the wild, where he has (spontaneously, it would appear) become a wolf, retaining the predatory character of the man he was. When Jupiter moves quickly back from the individual to punishing the race, the gods are reluctant, but Jupiter tells them to leave this to him: he will determine the proper manner of human destruction and even provide a better race of miraculous origin (1.209–52).

Teasingly, Ovid defers the expected flood narrative to explain that Jupiter would have used his thunderbolt if he had not recalled that it was fated that sea, earth, and sky would be scorched and the laboriously created cosmos endangered (is there a hint here that it had been *his* labor?) by fire. Instead, he chooses a different punishment: to drown mankind by sending rainstorms from all over the heavens.

In his narrative of the great flood Ovid ingeniously alternates vivid personifications of the participating supernatural powers: the rain-bearing south wind, the rainbow Iris, Neptune and his rampaging rivers, and later the Nereids and the sea god Triton. The thunderstorm is followed by rivers breaking their banks to gallop over the land, carrying off crops and orchards, cattle, peasants, their homes, and even the shrines of the gods (which would probably be the only stone structures in existence). Now Ovid has reversed creation, eliminating the distinction between earth and sea until there is nothing but sea, without any shoreline. In a series of paradoxes Ovid portrays the displacement of activities and creatures from land to sea, with seals basking on the hills, where formerly only goats grazed, and the sea nymphs marveling, not as they had in Catullus, at the first ship to cleave the waters, but at whole cities beneath the waves. The cataclysm levels all the creatures, so that

> Wolves swim among the sheep, and on the waters
> Tigers are borne along and tawny lions,
> No more his lightning stroke avails the boar
> Nor his legs the swift stag—both borne away.
> The wandering birds long seek a resting place,
> And drop with weary wings into the sea. (1.304–8,
>   tr. Melville)

As for humans, most are swept away, and those who escape the waves slowly starve to death. But Jupiter had promised a miracle. What form will it take?

This is in fact a Greek flood, and one mountain peak, holy Parnassus, towering over what would become Delphi, stayed above the waves. Now a pious old couple, Deucalion, son of Prometheus, with his wife and cousin, Pyrrha, land there in their little boat near the Corycian cave and oracle of Themis, the embodiment of divine justice. Once Jupiter sees that only these two good folk have survived, he scatters the rain clouds and uses the north wind to drive the storms away. On the sea too Neptune calms the waters and bids Triton sound the retreat for the rivers on his giant conch shell. There is instant obedience, and the sea recovers its shoreline, the rivers sink back within their beds, the hills emerge, and the forests again show their treetops, still coated with sludge.

Ovid makes clear the meaning of this moment. The earth was restored—but it was a desolate solitude. The pious old man addresses his wife, and together they ritually cleanse themselves in the river Cephisus and consult the divine Themis, whose shrine is still discolored with slime and mud. They recognize that what has happened comes from the anger of the gods, and they ask for mercy and a means to restore the lost human race. The oracle gives a suitably oracular answer: they must veil themselves and loosen their clothes and throw the bones of their great mother behind them.

Pyrrha, the wife, is more literal-minded and begs to be excused from insulting her mother's shade. Deucalion (naturally) is first to guess the goddess's meaning, that earth itself is their great mother and the stones are her bones. The stones that they cast behind them soften and begin to put on a shape (*forma* again). As they develop and ripen, they begin to take on a sort of human form, not obvious but like that of a statue just begun. Here is the most amazing of all metamorphoses, as nature is compared to the sculptor's art. So now the moister part of the stones turns into flesh, the hard stuff into bones, and the veins into—veins! And very shortly the rocks thrown by the man become men, and those thrown by the woman become women. This, Ovid explains, is why we are now such a hard race, enduring toil to prove our origin in stone (1.384–415).

But animal creation had also been destroyed. This is renewed by earth, unasked and unaided, as the sun warms the settling mud, and as dung and marsh grow hot and fertile seeds develop as if in a womb and take on recognizable shapes. To lend plausibility to this fantasy Ovid compares the worms and other creatures that Egyptian farmers find in the shallows of the receding Nile, many of them incomplete and limbless, some still half animal and half clods of earth. There is a close resemblance to Lucretius's account of animal incubation from the earth in his fifth book, even to the notion of some new forms being abortive or monstrous. The analogy with the mudflats of the Nile is known from Hellenistic tradition, and Ovid's imitation of Lucretian physics invokes a formula based on the opposing elements of fire and water: echoing his original creation he declares that their clashing combination (*discors concordia,* 433) was right for producing offspring. So now earth produced countless creatures, both old shapes (*figuras*) and new. Thus, while Ovid prefers to enhance the new creation of humanity by comparison with (human) artistry, he resorts to natural science and the theory of elements for the re-creation of animals. And, with this, Ovid is on his way to the story of the new monster Python, which is finally slain by Apollo. But our interest is more global, if not cosmic.

Phaethon's Fiery Ride

Greek and Roman tradition alike associated the two forms of world destruction—by flood and by fire—and followed the myth of Deucalion with that of Phaethon, the sun child, and the conflagration of heaven and earth caused by his disastrous ride in the sun chariot. In Plato's *Timaeus* Solon tells the story of Deucalion and the flood to the Egyptian priests as one of the oldest Greek myths, and an Egyptian replies that they know as well as the Greeks how Phaethon drove the sun chariot off-course and burnt up all the earth, until he perished, struck by Zeus's thunderbolt (*Tim.* 22a–c). For Lucretius it is obvious that the world must be destroyed from time to time by warring elements: the sun would consume everything if the rivers did not threaten to flood. Hence the ancient myth: "once at least the fire overwhelmed everything when the staggering force of the sun's horses swept Phaethon through all the skies and lands: then the almighty father in fierce anger thrust down the ambitious Phaethon with a sudden shock of thunder from his horses down to earth, and the sun, going to meet him as he fell, took up the world's eternal torch" (Lucr. 5.396–402).

Ovid's narrative sets the cosmic catastrophe in an amazing contrast of visual splendor and psychological frailty as he follows Phaethon to the dazzling palace of his father. On its doors are represented in silver all that the sun himself surveys: the seas encircling the earth, and the heaven hanging over the globe of the earth. Each element is full of life. The sea gods Triton, Proteus, and Aegaeon travel astride the whales, and the daughters of Doris swim or groom their hair. On earth are all the things that the flood once drowned: men and cities, woods and beasts, and rivers with nymphs and country spirits. Above the earth is engraved the gleaming sky, with six signs of the zodiac on each door. The ordered symmetry of this approach is repeated inside, where the courtiers of the Sun surround his emerald-studded throne. But these are personifications of time, not space: Day and Month and Year and the Ages are arrayed to left and right, and the Hours are stationed at intervals, while Spring, Summer, Autumn, and Winter stand beside the throne. When the Sun greets Phaethon as his child, taking off his radiate crown so Phaethon can embrace him, he invites his son to ask him a favor as pledge of his fatherly love. It is now that Phaethon demands the fatal chariot ride, and the sun god is trapped by his own promise. Ovid may have based both the Sun's eloquent speech of dissuasion and Phaethon's course through the zodiac in the messenger narrative of Euripides' tragedy *Phaethon*, which reported the sun god's warnings and the boy's departure. Certainly, Ovid's sun god warns the boy urgently of the superhuman strength required to resist the contrary motion of the heavens, to ascend in the face of the Bull and Lion, the Scorpion and Crab, and to control the fire-breathing horses. But his wise words are completely obliterated by the sight of the chariot, wrought by Vulcan in gold and silver.

As passionate fans of chariot racing, the Romans would share Phaethon's excitement. Ovid reinforces the image of the starting gate of the circus, when the Sun is urged on by the coming of Dawn as the stars recede. As the Hours yoke the champing horses, the Sun rubs Phaethon with a protective ointment and sets his crown upon him; accepting the inevitable, he now concentrates on warning the boy to keep close to the middle course. Much that he says echoes Nestor's warning to his son in the Homeric chariot race and will be repeated when another father, Daedalus, has to instruct his human son on his flight path in book 8.

Phaethon gleefully takes the reins, and the horses are released from their starting gate. As they sense the absence of weight and authority and swerve out of control, their driver does not know the way nor does he have the power to steer them, and the Arctic constellations shrink away to escape the heat. Looking down at earth below dazzles Phaethon, helpless to wield the reins. Only when he drops them in terror at the sprawling claws of the Scorpion (a constellation so large it occupied two sectors of the sky) do the horses break into a gallop (Ovid reuses the word he applied to the galloping flood streams), lurching ever nearer the earth, which cracks with the scorching heat, as cities, mountains, and forests burn. Whereas the flood, though traditionally universal, was associated in Ovid's (Greek) myth only with places in Greece, the fires consume all the mountain ranges around the Aegean, as far north as Scythia, and the peaks of Aetna and Eryx in Sicily. The sun would naturally travel westward, and Ovid lists, as the last ranges to suffer, the Alps and Apennines (2.226). But no region is spared. As Phaethon can no longer bear the rising flames or see through the smoke, the heat turns the Ethiopians black and makes Libya a desert. Rivers and springs dry up or retreat underground, and again Ovid's worldwide list reaches far beyond Greece to the Crimea and India, to Spain and Egypt and Thrace, ending in the western streams of the Rhine and Rhône and Po and even the Tiber (2.278–9). Driving deep into the earth, the heat terrifies the rulers of the underworld, and the sea creatures and even the naiad daughters of Doris take refuge underwater. Everything that was shown in its glory on the great palace doors is now damaged or at risk.

It is not known what moment provoked Jupiter's thunderbolt in earlier versions of this nightmare ride, though there was clearly a version as in Plato where Jupiter struck Phaethon in midcourse, allowing the Sun to take over an undamaged chariot. Ovid may be the first to introduce the protests of Mother Earth, as both ground and goddess, afflicted with tremors. Shrinking back into herself, she protests to Jupiter on behalf of land and sea and even sky (2.290–5). The climax of her speech is recognition that this is a return to the chaos before creation. Declaring that he must act or all creation will perish, Jupiter strikes down the charioteer with his thunderbolt. Panicking, the horses break from their yoke, leaving fragments of the chariot scattered across the earth. We who have grieved over so many crashed space shuttles and airliners have no difficulty in imagining a disaster that would have surpassed the experience of audiences in the Roman circus.

But a large part of the myth of Phaethon was concerned with the aftermath. While later accounts associated his fall with the mysterious Eridanus (a western river identified by Virgil with the Italian Po), other versions, such as Euripides' tragedy, had him born and perish nearer the sunrise—in the East. Since Ovid wanted to incorporate elements from both traditions, he separated the fate of chariot and rider. For him the Eridanus is Italian, and he holds his narrative to its banks. After the river received Phaethon's corpse and bathed his charred features, the naiads buried him with an inscription honoring him for the nobility of his ambition. His mother sought him across the whole world and found his bones there, buried in foreign soil. His sisters also came, and they wept there for four months until they went through a slow metamorphosis into poplar trees. As their mother tried to release them from the rising bark, they cried in pain and said their last farewells. But this transformation had a lasting effect that still benefits Ovid's culture: henceforward, the tree maidens' tears were amber, carried downstream to become wedding gifts for Latin brides. In another metamorphosis Phaethon's maternal kinsman Cycnus came there to lament, until he was transformed into a swan, which appropriately shuns flight and the dangers of the sky, haunting the river where his beloved died. This accumulation of human sorrow has led away from the cosmic scale of the disaster and results in a second, conflicting variant of the Sun's mourning for his child. Earlier, Ovid made the Sun refuse to shine for a whole day (in which the only light came from brushfires, 2.329–32); now Ovid has the Sun's protests overridden by Jupiter (2.381–400), who compels him to muster his team and drive them away—in the chariot which we know to be beyond repair. The world must resume, and the poet rounds off his tragedy with a touch of irony, as the Sun shifts blame for the disaster from gods and men (or parents and child) onto the fiery horses of the sky.

Further Reading

On Ovid's account of creation, see T. M. Robinson, "Ovid and the *Timaeus*," *Athenaeum* 46 (1968): 254–60; R. McKim, "Myth and Philosophy in Ovid's Account of Creation," *Classical Journal* 80 (1985): 97–108; M. Helzle, "Ovid's Cosmogony: *Metamorphoses* 1.5–88 and the Traditions of Ancient Poetry," *Papers of the Leeds Latin Seminar* 7 (1993): 123–34; Stephen M. Wheeler, "*Imago Mundi*: Another View of the Creation in Ovid's *Metamorphoses*," *American Journal of Philology* 116 (1995): 95–121; R. J. Tarrant, "Chaos in Ovid's *Metamorphoses* and Its Neronian Influence," in *Reception of Ovid in Antiquity*, ed. Garth Tissol and Stephen M. Wheeler, *Arethusa* 35 (2002). On flood and fire, see K. S. Myers, *Ovid's Causes: Cosmogony and Aetiology in Ovid's Metamorphoses* (Ann Arbor, 1994); on the Phaethon tradition, see J. Diggle, ed., *Euripides, "Phaethon"* (Cambridge, 1970).

·3·

Cadmus and the Tragic
Dynasty of Thebes

In the last chapter our focus on the natural world rather detracted from Ovid's lively characterization of men and gods, but toward the end of book 2 Ovid turns to the history of a human family, the Cadmean dynasty of Thebes, whose sufferings he depicts in recognizably tragic form. The story begins with another of Jupiter's seductions, presented as a sort of mirror image of his rape of Io. This time he himself becomes a handsome young bull in order to abduct the princess Europa from the seashore of Tyre. Teasingly, Ovid ends book 2 without closure as she sits astride the divine bull and has just realized that he is putting out to sea: we see only her panic, as she glances back to the shore, her clothes rippling in the sea breezes. As book 3 opens Jupiter discards his animal disguise on the shores of Crete, and Ovid passes on, suppressing Europa's rape and the birth of Minos. (Minos will enter the poem when he wages war on Aegina and Megara: see 7.456–60; 8.6–7.) It is Europa's brother Cadmus who is now the narrative focus, sent out by an angry father to find his sister—or remain an exile. Sensibly, he consults Apollo's oracle (established at Delphi in book 1), which instructs him to found a city by following an undomesticated cow until she chooses to rest.

When she settles, he sends his men to fetch water for a thanksgiving sacrifice to Jupiter.

But their search in the primeval forest disturbs a terrible serpent, protégé of Mars, with glittering golden crest, fiery eyes, threefold tongue, and triple rows of fangs, who rears up and attacks them:

> coil by scaly coil
> The serpent wound its way, and rearing up
> Curved in a giant arching bow, erect
> For more than half its length, high in the air.
> It glared down on the whole wide wood as huge,
> If all its size were seen, as in the sky
> The Snake that separates the two bright Bears.
> Then in a trice it seized them, some in flight,
> Some set to fight, some fixed too fast in fear
> For either. Every man of them it slew,
> With fang that struck or coil that crushed, or breath
> That dealt a putrid blast of poisoned death. (3.41–9,
> tr. Melville)

Cadmus goes searching for them but does not find them until sunset, when he discovers the serpent feasting on its victims. His first attack with a boulder only enrages it and it tramples the forest, until Cadmus ends the struggle with a spear-throw that drives through its jaw and pins it to an oak tree. Foreshadowing what will be the last moment of Ovid's "Theban cycle," a supernatural voice warns him that as penalty he too will become a serpent. Acting on the advice of Pallas Athene, he plows the earth to sow the serpent's teeth: slowly a crop of warriors emerge headfirst like painted figures on a Roman theater curtain (which was stored below stage level, exposing its figures as it rose). Once grown to full height they attack each other in civil war. Again the earth is hot with the fresh bloodshed of a new creation, but when only five of these "Sown Men" are left, one of them, Echion, initiates peace. With the five, Cadmus founds his new city, a counterpart of Rome in its genesis in civil war and association with Mars.

The inhuman origin of the Sown Men contributes to the ill-fortune of Cadmus's city and dynasty, which Ovid unfolds in four major episodes, one for each of his four daughters (despite 3.134, no sons are recorded). Of these Agave marries Echion and is the mother of Pentheus. Cadmus has another grandson, Actaeon, by his daughter Autonoe and also has grandchildren by his daughter Ino, wife of Athamas. Only Semele is unmarried; she is courted by Jupiter, and that stormy union will result in the premature birth of the god Bacchus/Dionysus. Within book 3 Ovid includes three terrible and spectacular deaths: of Actaeon, Semele, and finally Pentheus, punished for his persecution of Bacchus. In book 4, after some diversionary tales of love told by women who resist the worship of Bacchus, Cadmus's last daughter, Ino, is driven mad by Juno and ends her mortal life by leaping from a cliff.

Now although Ovid makes it very clear that Cadmus founds his city by divine command (3.130–1), there is no description of its walls, forum, temples, and palace; in fact, almost every Theban crisis occurs in the wild, which is also the setting of the two most extended diversionary tales in these books. Indeed, the city walls and dwellings, so prominent when the women abandon their homes in Euripides' *Bacchae,* are mentioned only once in this whole book (in Pentheus's speech at 3.550).

To quote a recent study (Gildenhard and Zissos 1999: 1711), "the importance of seeing and being seen emerges as a prominent theme in almost every episode of book 3, starting with Actaeon." The young hunter, introduced as "Cadmus's first bereavement" (3.138), has enjoyed a successful morning slaughtering many animals on the hillside when he decides to call off the hunt at noon. Tradition had made him one of those boasters who provoke divine fury by claiming to be more skillful than the gods—in this case, the huntress Diana. Instead, Ovid presents Actaeon's offense as an accident—more a blunder than a crime. Like Cadmus's retainers he stumbles into danger. The poet evokes one of those exquisite woodland scenes that promise repose and conceal lurking tragedy (Segal 1969): a grotto in which nature has surpassed art, creating a grassy-edged pool where Diana has come to bathe after hunting. While one nymph combs Diana's hair, five take turns pouring water over the goddess. When Actaeon appears, they cry out, forming a circle around Diana, whose blush is emphasized by rich similes (3.183–5; compare the blush of Hermaphroditus, 4.329–33). Since her arrows are out of reach, she strikes him with a splash of water and curses him: "now go and tell others that you saw me naked—if you can" (192–3).

It is not enough that this turns Actaeon into a stag, depriving him of speech but not of human consciousness (3.194–205). His hounds catch sight of this new prey, and they are a numerous pack. Ovid names thirty-three before he grows tired, but the hounds that actually bring Actaeon down are three previously unnamed, Black-pelt, Beastkiller, and Hillbred, who took a shortcut to overtake the others. Such circumstantial details simply increase the horror as Ac-taeon, their master, tries to cry out, and his followers urge on the hounds, indignant that he is not there to watch, while he "who would have gladly been anywhere else" (247) is torn apart alive; only then is Diana's anger appeased.

Cadmus's family will suffer, and also inflict, another horribly simi-lar divine vengeance, but first Ovid must explain the extraordinary birth of Cadmus's grandson Bacchus (3.259–315). We are not told how Jupiter became Semele's lover, only that Juno hated her, jeal-ous of Jupiter's mating first with her aunt Europa and now Semele. Angry that Semele is pregnant, the goddess (who never had a satis-factory child of her own) determines to use her husband to cause the girl's death. She approaches Semele disguised as her old nurse, urging her to test her lover. Just as Phaethon caused his own death by exacting a blank promise from his father as proof of love, so now the "nurse" persuades Semele to ask Jupiter to prove his love by let-ting her see him in the full form with which he makes love to Juno. Even though the god resorts to a second-grade thunderbolt (Ovid loves to play on technology), his coming consumes Semele with fire, but he saves her fetus, inserting it into his own thigh until ges-tation is completed: "if it can be believed," says the poet (311), de-murring at this switch of gender role and so distancing his readers from his own narrative. Once born, the baby Bacchus is nursed by his aunt Ino and then given to the nymphs to rear out of Juno's sight.

Readers would now be ready to hear the famous tragedy of Bacchus's divine return to Thebes, but Ovid defers this climax by introducing the figure of the prophet Teiresias in a remarkably compact flashback (3.318–38). This digression offers a fine sample of Ovid's complex skill at coloring a tale with unexpected tone and phrase. For a start, this is not the stern Teiresias who brings terror to Oedipus and his successors, but a mere mortal consulted by a Jupiter mellow with ambrosia after Juno contradicted his claim that women derived more pleasure from sex than men. Ovid calls it a joke, but Juno was notoriously deprived of her conjugal rights (witness the trouble she must take to get Jupiter to sleep with her in *Iliad* 14). Why call on Teiresias? Because, in Ovid's version, Teiresias had enjoyed both the male and the female experience of intercourse, since he had passed seven years as a woman after undergoing metamorphosis when he struck two serpents mating in a wood. Only by repeating the attack when he next saw the serpents was he able to return to masculinity (323–31). The joke has become a legal dispute, with Teiresias formally dignified as arbiter. When he decides in favor of Jupiter (Ovid's language is legalistic), Juno, like Diana (333–4 cf. 253), acts unjustly: she sentences him to eternal blindness. What can Jupiter do? Ovid enunciates the relevant theological principle in recognizably legal terms: since one god may not overturn another's ruling, Jupiter can only compensate for this deprivation of sight by giving Teiresias expertise in the future. By a perversion of legal procedure, it is the arbiter who suffers a penalty.

The experiences of Teiresias link him thematically with Cadmus in three ways: through the woodland, the serpents, and the element of prophecy. Echoing the last motif, Ovid builds his account around the fulfillment of two of Teiresias's prophecies: one to Narcissus's mother, Liriope, the other to Cadmus's surviving human grandson, Pentheus. But let us postpone the extended case history of Narcissus and instead follow Pentheus and the fortunes of the house of Cadmus.

Only Pentheus, called son of Echion (3.513) to remind the reader of his inhuman ancestry, feels no respect for the gods and ignores and insults Teiresias. Pentheus mocks him as blind; "So I am," says Teiresias, "and you would be happier if you too were blind, so as not to see the rites of Bacchus." To give this prophetic warning greater weight, Ovid confronts Pentheus and his readers with direct speech, foretelling his death by laceration, defiling the woods and his own mother and her sisters.

The coming of Bacchus is the high point of Ovid's narrative, strongly colored by Euripides' *Bacchae.* At Rome itself the senate had seen the cult of Bacchus as so uncontrollable and dangerous to communal order that they had banned its public observation two hundred years before Ovid's death. Euripides' play presents the madness of female bacchantes as something both exalting and terrible and derives its *pathos* (tragic crisis) from the god's vengeance on his own natal family: not only the destruction of Pentheus, who openly persecuted Bacchus, but the ruin and shame of the aunts who denied his divine birth. Ovid clearly admired Euripides but varied his account to adapt the dramatic form to his epic context. To keep the focus on Pentheus, he passes over the chorus of Bacchantes and the messengers' marvelous descriptions of their rituals in the mountain wilderness. Ovid also eliminates the prologue, in which the god boasts of driving the women out from the city, and plays down the role of Cadmus, who made young Pentheus ruler of Thebes but now goes with Teiresias to welcome Bacchus. Instead, Ovid's highly wrought narrative begins with an impassioned speech by Pentheus scorning the cult as effeminate while urging his dragon-born warriors to defend Thebes against this degenerate invasion and arrest its leader (3.527–63). The protests of Cadmus and other princes only increase his perverse determination.

Euripides had brought Dionysus into the action in person, thinly concealing his identity as the captured leader: in two increasingly sinister scenes he played with young Pentheus and gained psychological control of him. Instead, Ovid adapts a post-Euripidean tragedy, the *Pentheus* of Pacuvius, in which the king takes captive a follower of Bacchus who identifies himself as the sailor Acoetes, an unwilling accomplice of Tyrrhenian pirates who tried to abduct the young god and were punished for it. The climax of Acoetes' narrative is the miracle briefly celebrated in the Homeric hymn to Dionysus but now expanded into a wonderful tale that again defers the coming crisis. Acoetes takes thirty lines just to explain how he became a steersman and how he put in at Chios. Next he introduces his fellow sailors (naming eight of them!) and the richly dressed half-tipsy boy they pick up on the shore, whose divinity he guesses. Some fifty lines combining narrative and direct dialogue (605–55) portray the sailors' mutiny as they seize the helm from Acoetes and abduct the young passenger, steering course away from his destination. At that moment the young god switches suddenly from pathetic protests to supernatural action. As in the Homeric hymn, Acoetes describes the ship becalmed, tendrils of ivy entangling the oars and dragging down the sails with grape clusters, while the garlanded god brandishes a spear entwined with vine leaves. In the hymn Dionysus produced a lion and a bear to terrify the sailors; Ovid has tigers and "unreal images of lynxes and wild bodies of spotted panthers"—making it clear that the beasts are phantoms. In horror the sailors leap into the sea, and the poet lingers over their transformation into dolphins; a close paraphrase will show his vivid specificity (671–86):

> Medon turns black and is curved around his protruding spine, Lycabas's mouth splits into a wide grinning jaw and snout as he jeers and his skin hardens into scales, while Libys at the oars sees his arms turn to fins; another man at the rigging loses his arms and leaps, curving backward into the sea, growing a forked tail like a crescent moon. Finally, they form a dolphin school, playing and frisking and blowing seawater from their spreading nostrils.

When Acoetes ends with the god's reassurance and his own conversion to worship of Bacchus, Pentheus cuts him off and has him dragged away to be tortured in prison. The narrative accelerates to convey the god's power as doors open and chains fall away from the prisoner (3.692–700).

Was Acoetes a human worshiper or Bacchus himself? He disappears from Ovid's narrative, and Pentheus goes of his own accord to Cithaeron, reacting to the women's howling like a warhorse that hears the bugle. Omitting Euripides' details of transvestism and concealment, Ovid stresses the openness of the setting, like a Roman amphitheater ready for a wild-beast hunt; but this hunt will have a human prey. When Pentheus is spotted observing the sacred action with profane eyes, it is his mother who sees him first, and sees him as an animal, summoning her sisters to kill the wild boar; as the mob descends on him he supplicates his aunt Autonoe in the name of her dead son, Actaeon, but the women now take over the hideous role of Actaeon's hounds. In their maenad state Autonoe and Ino pull off his arms; his last appeal is to his mother, who tears off his head and holds it aloft to her companions as proof of victory. Where Euripides ended with an extended scene of pathos as Cadmus struggles to make his daughter realize what she has done, Ovid brings the dreadful story to a quiet close with a simile: "the wind does not blow leaves loosened by the autumn frost more swiftly from a lofty tree than the man's limbs were torn apart by abominable hands" (3.729–31).

Now indeed Bacchus's rites are celebrated by the women of Thebes. But Juno is not appeased, and there will be an aftermath. Once his readers are gripped by concern for the doomed dynasty, Ovid deliberately interrupts his main narrative to divert them with the sufferings and metamorphoses of private individuals. Why does he do this, and how do the misadventures of Narcissus and Echo in book 3 and the three very different stories told by the Minyeides in book 4 reflect on the main Theban narrative and on each other? One common element is the antithesis between the man-made domestic world of the city and the untamed outdoors.

We have learned from the rape of Io (not to mention Daphne and Callisto) that the countryside is dangerous, especially where the landscape tempts with pleasant refuge from heat and thirst by a shady pool. The diversionary tales of book 4 will show that, like Semele's charred bedchamber, the home can be as dangerous as the wilderness and will illustrate the troubles attendant on different forms of love. Since these include the two best-known "tales of Ovid"—the lovesick death of Narcissus and the shared fate of the lovers Pyramus and Thisbe—they cannot be passed over. When Jupiter planned to destroy mankind he wanted to make the world safe for demigods and nymphs. We may not notice it, but most of the girl victims in the early books are nymphs, either daughters of rivers like Daphne and Io, companions of Diana, or independent nymphs like Cyane and Arethusa in book 5. One such is Liriope, who consults Teiresias about the future of her son, Narcissus, and is told (in a reversal of the Delphic saying "know thyself") that "he will be happy if he never knows himself." Another is Echo, who falls foul of Juno by distracting her with gossip so that she will not catch Jupiter chasing other nymphs. Juno in turn punishes Echo by depriving her of independent speech: she can only repeat (and so usually agree with) what is said by others around her. Thus, the nymph is reduced to the "supporting" role that many Romans thought proper to women (3.359–69). The fates of Narcissus and Echo converge when the young man, now a handsome sixteen-year-old who has rejected many admirers, goes hunting. Echo falls in love with the youth and pursues him, apparently unseen, and unable to speak except to echo his words, which Ovid contrives so that they match her purpose. His dialogue stands near the beginning of what will become a long tradition of Echo poems. For once let us read both Ovid's Latin (Narcissus speaks in boldface letters, Echo in italics) as well as Melville's elegant English version:

> forte puer comitum seductus ab agmine fido
> dixerat **"ecquis adest?"** et *"adest!"* responderat Echo.
> hic stupet, utque aciem partes dimittit in omnes
> voce **"veni!"** magna clamat; vocat illa vocantem.
> respicit et rursus nullo veniente **"quid"** inquit
> **"me fugis?"** et totidem, quot dixit verba recepit.
> perstat et alternae deceptus imagine vocis
> **"huc coeamus!"** ait nullique libentius usque
> responsura sono *"coeamus"* rettulit Echo.
>   . . . .

. . . "ante," ait, "emoriar, quam sit tibi copia nostri."
rettulit illa nihil nisi *"sit tibi copia nostri!"* (3.379–87, 391–2)

It chanced Narcissus, searching for his friends,
Called "Anyone here?" and Echo answered "Here!"
Amazed he looked around and raised his voice,
Called "Come this way!" and Echo called "This way!"
He looked behind, and no one coming, shouted
"Why run away?" and heard his words again.
He stopped and, cheated by the answering voice,
Called "Join me here" and she, never more glad
To give her answer, answered "Join me here!"
. . . .
. . . He bolted, shouting "Keep your arms from me!
Be off! I'll die before I yield to you."
And all she answered was "I yield to you." (3.379–87,
        390–92 tr. Melville)

It happens that one Latin word, *imago,* denotes both an echo—or
aural reflection—and a reflection, which we might conceive of as a
visual echo. Misled by the echo of his own voice (*imagine vocis,* 385),
Narcissus urges the unknown to come to meet him, but when Echo
emerges from hiding and he sees her approaching, he repels her.
Rejected, she hides and pines away in the woods until only her
voice is left to be heard (3.375–401).

The time comes when one of the many lovers Narcissus has rejected curses him—"so may he love and never win his love!"—and
Nemesis, as goddess of retribution, gives her approval. It is now that
Narcissus comes to drink at a cold pure spring whose surface no leaf
or creature has disturbed and sees reflected in it an image as lovely
as a statue of Parian marble (3.419; but it is Ovid, not Narcissus,
who is in love with statues; compare his images for Hermaphroditus, 4.354–5, and Andromeda, 4.673–5). Beguiled by this beautiful
reflection, he obsessively tries to touch the boy in the water; the
poet himself steps into the scene to scold Narcissus for his folly:
"you simple boy, why strive in vain to catch / a fleeting image? What
you see is nowhere / and what you love—but turn away—you lose"

(3.432–3, tr. Melville). Ovid loves paradoxes based on the opposition of illusion and reality and, like Narcissus, can hardly tear himself away from the fascinating situation. He constructs an extended soliloquy (442–62) in which the echoing words express the reflexivity of the boy's situation, until he realizes that he is gazing at himself and launches into a new sequence of complaints (463–73, 477–9).

Now it is his turn to pine and fade away, until the beauty that excited Echo has almost gone; but as he cries, "alas, the boy I loved in vain," she echoes, and truly means, his words, just as she echoes his last "farewell." The other nymphs beat their breasts and prepare to bury him, but only a flower is left, the white and golden narcissus.

Teiresias is vindicated, as he will be again by Pentheus's grim death, but amid general hymns of praise, some still resist the worship of the new god. The daughters of Minyas stay at home and refuse to join in welcoming Bacchus (4.31–41). Each offers the others a tale to accompany their spinning. The first is the bourgeois romance of the young Babylonian neighbors Pyramus and Thisbe (4.55–166). When their parents forbid them to meet, they whisper through the chink in the dividing wall made famous by Shakespeare's comic adaptation in *Midsummer Night's Dream* and arrange a rendezvous at Ninus's tomb outside the city. But Pyramus arrives late, after a lioness has already driven Thisbe away in flight. Finding her bloodstained scarf, he thinks her dead and kills himself. The metamorphosis in this tragedy occurs when the dying Pyramus pulls out his sword, and his spurting blood stains the white mulberries of the overhanging tree (almost) black. As for Thisbe, when she timidly returns and finds his body, she uses the discarded sword to join him in death. Here at last is an urban story, with the apparently clear messages that nothing is safe outside the city and love is prone to hasty but fatal errors.

The story of the second sister (based on a comic lay sung by the bard Demodocus in the *Odyssey*) brings danger indoors: it starts with a consequence of Vulcan's entrapment of his adulterous wife Venus and Mars by stretching invisible magic nets over the marital bed. Because it was the Sun who first spied the adultery and informed Vulcan, Venus wants vengeance and afflicts the Sun with passion for a princess, Leucothoe. Jupiter had raped Callisto by disguising himself as her mistress, the goddess Diana: the Sun goes one worse and disguises himself as poor Leucothoe's mother, raping her (though there is a hint that the girl is won over by the brilliance of his real solar form) as she is spinning in her own bedchamber (4.169–233). Nowhere is safe, but is the poet perhaps implying that the spinning Minyeides enjoy the thought of ubiquitous seduction?

The last story is both the strangest and the closest in theme and setting to Ovid's own narrative of Narcissus. It sets out to explain the origin of the sinister spring Salmacis, which supposedly emasculates those who swim in it. There actually was a spring of this name at Halicarnassus, which is celebrated in a surviving inscription in epic verse which praises its healing qualities. But Ovid chooses the more lurid version and even has Pythagoras list its vile waters (*obscenae . . . undae,* 15.319) among the miraculous springs and rivers of his *Natural History* (see ch. 8). Salmacis is another nymph, who does not even hunt but lazily bathes in her perfect pool, using its waters to reflect her appearance as she grooms her hair. She may be narcissistic, but sexually she is a nymphomaniac. When she catches sight of the beautiful boy Hermaphroditus (child of Venus and Mercury), she shamelessly accosts him. He blushes in horror, so she promises to withdraw but lurks until he has entered the pool. Now, one of Ovid's favorite forms of paradox is to play on the dual nature of water gods: a river will be at one minute a lustful male deity, then instantly a watery torrent. So Salmacis is her own pool, and when Hermaphroditus strips to bathe, the poet conveys her lust and his beauty through images that recall Narcissus and his fate: her eyes flash like a mirror image of the sun (347–9), we see the naked boy through her eyes like white lilies under glass or an ivory statue (354–5), and she entwines him like a snake or ivy or an octopus wrapping its tentacles all around (362–7). She begs the gods to unite them for ever, and they (most unfairly) grant her prayer, fusing the two bodies to make Hermaphroditus an effeminate "half-male." He in turn asks his divine parents to ensure that whoever shall bathe in these waters may emerge equally effeminate. The same combination of curses and prophecies animates this curiously odious story as that of Narcissus, and in each case the story serves to explain a natural phenomenon: the new flower or the drugged waters.

Ovid returns symmetrically to his main narrative with an indoor miracle to match Dionysus's transformation of the pirate ship. The women's home offers no more protection against the god than the wild outdoors. Now their looms grow green, turning into vines laden with grapes, and as twilight falls the house is filled with blazing torches and phantoms of howling wild beasts. Fleeing, the women seek dark corners and develop transparent membranes and the squeaky voice of bats, appearing in houses by night rather than in the Dionysiac woodland (407–15). Where Nicander's metamorphosis had made each sister into a different nocturnal creature, all three become Vespertiliones, taking their name from Vesper, the evening star.

Now indeed Bacchus is triumphant, and his foolish aunt Ino, the only sister still unharmed, boasts of his glory. In Greek legend, Ino and her husband, Athamas, were sent mad by a jealous Hera (Juno) and killed their own children. Ovid does not change their fate, but he borrows from Virgil to enrich Juno's supernatural action with echoes and allusions to Aeneas's journey through the underworld and to Juno's exploitation of the Fury Allecto in her vengeful assault on the Trojans in *Aeneid* 7; these supernatural, even hellish scenes had met with extraordinary admiration from public and poets alike. Ovid exploits both narrative elements, making Juno travel to Hades to find the Fury Tisiphone and send her to madden Athamas and Ino, as Tisiphone's sister Allecto had maddened Queen Amata and Turnus in the *Aeneid*. A miniature journey past the traditional sinners of Tartarus finds Tisiphone combing the serpents from her gray hair. Juno asks her to ensure that the monarchy of Cadmus will collapse and Athamas be driven to criminal acts (4.432–80). Tisiphone acts instantly and emerges aboveground with her retinue of horrors, infecting the atmosphere; like Virgil's Fury, she attacks Athamas with two venomous serpents which do him no physical harm but drive him to murder. Pausing to toss flaming torches around the house, she returns to Hades—mission accomplished (4.481–511). As Athamas kills his sons, Ino, either from grief or infected by the Fury, flees from their home clutching little Melicertes and howling Bacchic cries. But other gods intervene: as Ino leaps from a cliff, her grandmother Venus asks Neptune to rescue mother and child, and they acquire new names and forms as the marine gods Leucothea and Palaemon; even Ino's maids are transformed in a typical Ovidian postscript, into seabirds (543–62).

Ovid returns at last to Cadmus, who believes all his children are dead, not knowing that Ino and his grandson are now divine. Overwhelmed by successive calamities and believing the place itself is doomed, he resolves to leave the city he has founded. The story has come full circle as he and his wife, Harmonia, wander in exile to the lands of Illyria. In Euripides' *Bacchae* Dionysus had appeared to Cadmus promising him a future as leader of an Illyrian tribe before he and Harmonia were finally transformed into snakes. This would fulfill the prophecy of the mysterious voice heard by Cadmus when he founded Thebes, that "he too would be seen in the form of a serpent." Outdoing his tragic model, Ovid presents what Euripides only foretold. As the couple reminisce, Cadmus prays that if his misfortunes come from divine anger, he may be turned into a crawling serpent. The transformation is made poignant, if slightly absurd, by the loving distress of his wife, as he seeks to climb into her arms and lick her face; she in turn strokes his slithery serpent neck and they are entwined in mutual coils and retreat together into the shady woods. Even now, says Ovid, these serpents do not shun or harm men but gently recall the humans they once were. The misfortunes of Thebes did not end with the house of Cadmus, but Ovid has brought his narrative of the earliest Greek city and royal house to a comforting closure: he will not return there until the generation of Hercules.

Further Reading

For Ovid's treatment of Thebes as counterpart of Rome, see P. R. Hardie, "Ovid's Theban History: The First 'Anti-*Aeneid*'?" *Classical Quarterly* 40 (1990): 224–35; A. Feldherr, "Metamorphosis and

Sacrifice in Ovid's Theban Narrative," *Materiali e Discussioni* 38 (1997): 25–55. On Narcissus, see C. P. Segal, *Landscape in Ovid's "Metamorphoses": A Study in the Transformation of a Literary Symbol* (Wiesbaden, 1969); P. R. Hardie, *Ovid's Poetics of Illusion* (Cambridge, 2002); I. Gildenhard and A. Zissos, "Somatic Economies: Tragic Bodies and Poetic Design in Ovid's *Metamorphoses*," in *Ovidian Transformations: Essays on the "Metamorphoses" and Its Reception,* ed. Philip Hardie, Alessandro Barchiesi, and Stephen Hinds (Cambridge, 1999), 162–81. On the influence of tragedy, see A. Keith, "Sources and Genres in Ovid's *Metamorphoses* 1–5," in *Brill's Companion to Ovid*, ed. B. W. Boyd (Leiden, 2002), 235–69 (at 263–9).

·4·

Human Artistry and Divine Jealousy

Ovid has already made clear the egotism and vindictiveness of the Olympian gods, who cannot endure a human rival. But their jealousy is not confined to sexual matters, and the poet will demonstrate repeatedly how human artists are punished, or simply victimized, for challenging a god's professional expertise. In this context, it does not matter whether their performance succeeds or fails: to compete with a god on any terms brings loss of human identity. Among the five tales of divinely imposed metamorphosis in books 5–6, three are of formal contests and illustrate how human musicians and artists compete with divine beings and suffer for it.

Ovid's first example is so extended that one competition piece displaces the main text. When Pallas Athene comes to Helicon to see Hippocrene, the fountain created by the winged horse Pegasus, she graciously congratulates the Muses, daughters of Memory, on their skill and the amenities of their new home. Suddenly there is a beating of wings and the sound of birds—nine magpies—uttering recognizable human greeting. The Muse Urania explains that these are the daughters of Pieros and Euippe, only freshly turned into birds after being defeated in a song contest. Here the poet teases his

readers, since this parentage would make these human sisters Pierides, a name regularly given to the Muses themselves; but he has
found and exploited a variant myth in Nicander and will call the
Muses by other names through this long episode. We are told that
the sisters challenged the Muses to a song contest, boasting that they
would not be outdone in singing or artistry. Their spokeswoman
proposed that if the sisters won, the Muses should resign claim to
the fountain, but if they lost, the sisters would leave the region altogether. In this and other contests it seems to be assumed that the
losers must pay a penalty, though this was not the pattern in Greek
games. It is also the practice (as in Virgil's pastoral song contests)
that the challenger names a judge, and if this judge is accepted by
the other contestant they proceed. We are told that the Pierides demanded the nymphs as judges; the formalities were observed and
the nymphs sworn in before taking their seats.

How much can Ovid convey of the rival performances? His audience, of course, can measure only the quality of the written text
offered by the poet. But this would be only one of the four skills
tested in such competitions. Whether the poetic genre was lyric or
epic (and this will be epic), the same person was poet and composer,
singer and accompanist on the lyre: in *mousike*, the Greek art of song,
the one artist both created and then performed words and music.
This was the art of the citharode, invented by Apollo, who will put
in a professional appearance later in this chapter and Ovid's poem.
On this occasion, Ovid does not report the competition in person
but leaves it to the Muse, a party we may suspect of some bias. She
begins by summarizing the song of the leading Pierid sister—who
apparently narrated the wars of the giants against the Olympians,
giving false credit to the giants and belittling the gods' heroism. The
Pierid even claimed that Typhoeus put the gods to flight as far as
Egypt—and at this point the Muse reproduces her words:

> "and Jove became a ram,"
> She said, "Lord of the herd, and so today
> Great Libyan Ammon's shown with curling horns,
> Phoebus hid as a raven, Bacchus a goat,

Phoebe a cat, Juno a snow-white cow,
Venus a fish, and Mercury an ibis" (5.327–31, tr. Melville)

The song seems rather perfunctory, but despite the historically correct equation of Greek and Egyptian deities, it was clearly offensive in its blasphemous content. Next, it is the turn of the Muses, again represented by one sister, Calliope. Encouraged by Athene, Calliope produces a complete miniature epic (5.341–661) on the rape of Persephone by Dis and Ceres' search. Of course, Ovid has given it all his narrative skill and incorporated a feminist perspective to appeal to the nymph-judges; male gods are lustful or untrustworthy, and human males are rude or treacherous; only the nymphs Cyane and Arethusa are loyal and helpful. The judges unanimously declare for the Muses. In anger the defeated Pierides turn to abuse and are punished for being bad losers by transformation into magpies as noisy and garrulous as the girls themselves had been.

Tapestry: The Feminine Art

The story leads Athene to think about her own prestige and the praise and thanks that are her due as inventor and teacher of weaving. She is angered that the young weaver Arachne, born of a humble family, is supposedly her match in skill. Indeed, the nymphs would desert their streams not just to see her completed tapestries but to observe her in action—carding, spinning, and weaving. Arachne is so skilled, says the poet editorially, that you would know she had learnt from Pallas Athene, but she denies it and issues a challenge, declaring that she is willing to pay any forfeit if she loses (6.1–25). When Athene accosts her disguised as an old woman, she persists in her disrespect until Athene reveals her identity and imposes a contest between them. This time Ovid gives both contestants equal treatment, first describing how they work at speed to set up their looms, "moving their expert arms, as their dedicated concentration makes the toil pass unnoticed" (6.59–60). Indeed, his magical description of subtle rainbow shading is applied to both webs alike.

He describes the goddess's tapestry first (suggesting that it will be outdone by her rival): it is self-congratulatory, if not also self-fulfilling, representing her previous victory over Neptune when they competed before the other gods for patronage of Athens. Ovid describes twelve gods in ceremonial symmetry on either side of Jupiter (but this is problematic: Athene and Neptune are competing before ten others!). She shows Neptune striking the earth with his trident, and the fountain emerging, then herself, fully armed, striking the earth, from which emerges a tree loaded with olives: the gods marvel and her work produces victory. Then to warn her rival she weaves in each of the four corners an example of those who foolishly competed with the gods and suffered metamorphosis. Finally, she surrounds its edges with olive branches and marks the end of her work with the foliage of her tree (6.70–102).

Arachne's theme is also metamorphosis, but in an aesthetically daring and morally scandalous form: first, she illustrates Europa deceived by Jupiter as the bull, "so vividly you would think it a real bull and real seas" (the reader too would have been deceived!); Europa seems to be looking back to land (cf. 2.873) and calling to her companions and shrinking from the leaping waves. But this is only one of more than twenty scenes of women raped by Jupiter, Neptune, Apollo, Bacchus, and Saturn, each god shown only in the animal or material disguise adopted for his sexual purpose: Jupiter, for example, appears to Danae (and Arachne's spectators) as gold, and to Tyro as fire, while Bacchus seduces Erigone in the form of a bunch of grapes. To complete her canvas, the last part of the web is surrounded with a delicate border of ivy interwoven with entwining flowers.

Ovid does not indicate how these scenes were arranged on the tapestry, though modern critics suggest a swirling spiral, which would certainly be a technical challenge. Instead, the poet implies her success by affirming that it leaves nothing for Pallas to fault. Envy itself could not criticize the work of art, but the goddess, in her jealousy, tears apart her rival's cloth and strikes Arachne with her shuttle. The girl tries to hang herself in bitter indignation, but Athene crowns her injustice by shrinking Arachne into a spider, which spins threads from its belly, still weaving her webs as she did in the past. To this reader at least, the destruction of Arachne's masterpice seems more terrible than the ensuing metamorphosis. If Athene were not a goddess, we would call this a tantrum, and the poet shares the popular indignation that he reports: even if all artists are conceived as learning from divine skill, Ovid sees the outcome as beyond justification by Arachne's pride or ingratitude.

Here is a consummate artist of humble origin, acknowledging no debts for her artistry and challenging authority by its contents, destroyed along with her masterpiece by a jealous authority figure. Could Arachne stand for Ovid himself, with Pallas playing Augustus (see Lateiner 1984)? Hardly, I think, unless he composed this scene after Augustus had sent him into exile by his personal decree. To have set up such an implicit analogy before the blow of exile would have been asking for the penalty Ovid actually suffered.

In the symbolism of literature, such woven tapestries have an importance beyond that common to all textiles as measure of a woman's skill. They are also the female counterpart to men's poetry. In the *Iliad,* Helen weaves tapestries narrating the events of the war, just as the hero Achilles sings to his lyre the narratives of former heroic deeds. But they are more than that. When the weavers are setting up their looms, the poet speaks of the ancient narrative (*argumentum,* 69) being laid down on the web, and the final border of Arachne's tapestry ends with the word translated as "interwoven" (*intertextos,* 128), evoking the affinity of woven design with written text, both constructed in rows across an existing tissue (papyrus was made of horizontal layers glued across vertical ones). The convergence of pictorial with written communication is most apparent in the secret message woven later in book 6 by the imprisoned Philomela, whose tongue has been cut out by her rapist. What she sends to alert her sister to her fate is a tapestry with signs woven in red on a ground of white, "evidence of the crime committed" (6.576–8). Procne "unrolls the cloth" (like a written scroll) and "reads the pitiable poem of her misfortune" (6.581). Has Philomela woven a written text or a visual depiction of her rape? In choosing the word "marks," or "signs" (*notae*) (6.577), Ovid may be recalling the secret message sent with Bellerophon at *Iliad* 6.168, bearing ominous *semata* (marks or signs) to ensure his execution. Like the contest, Philomela's message equates tapestry with text, but unlike Arachne's web, her message reverses the balance of power. There could be no stronger symbol of both the silencing of women and the compensation afforded by the written word, as Charles Segal has brought out in "Philomela's Web and the Pleasures of the Text" (1994).

Yet Ovid undoubtedly saw poetry in its full musical form as the highest art, and he expresses its power through two other musical contests and through the person and music of Orpheus. In book 11 Ovid portrays Apollo competing as citharode in full concert attire:

> Apollo's golden hair
> Was garlanded with laurel of Parnassus;
> His mantle, rich with Tyrian purple, swept
> The ground he trod; in his left hand he bore
> His lyre, inlaid with gems and ivory;
> His right the plectrum held, his very pose
> Proclaimed the artist. Then with expert touch
> He plucked the strings. (11.165–70, tr. Melville)

This is an unequal contest, as Ovid warns his readers, because Apollo is competing with Pan, whose instrument is only the reed pipes: a piper cannot sing but can only accompany another singer, so Pan produces only melody without words. But although Pan loses the contest, he is still a god and does not suffer; it is only the misguided critic Midas who is punished with a partial metamorphosis, growing asses' ears because he preferred the pipes. According to tradition, another piper, Marsyas the satyr, was brutally punished by Apollo for competing. But after the cruel tale of Niobe in book 6, Ovid has had enough of contests and of Apollo's vengeance. In sharp contrast he only briefly evokes Apollo's flaying of the satyr who dared to rival his music and subordinates Marsyas's protests (6.382–400) at divine injustice to the metamorphosis by which the tears shed for Marsyas's death became the Phrygian river that bears his name.

The Isolation of the Poet and Artist:
Orpheus and Pygmalion

Apollo was also father, by the Muse Calliope, of the singer-poet Orpheus, and the god's trivial contest with Pan comes only after Ovid has told the tragic story of Orpheus and his miraculous art. As the miniature epic of his mother, Calliope, occupied the second half of book 5, so the many poetic tales of Orpheus fill book 10. As a poet's epic his song sequence will be analyzed later in its own right, but since Orpheus was always the model of the supreme artist, we should pause here to notice how simply Ovid conveys the emotional power of his artistry, not with elaborate detail of the performance, but by reporting its effect on even inhuman listeners. When Orpheus descends to Hades to plead for the restoration of Eurydice, the dead souls weep at his words, as he plucks his lyre; tormented sinners pause from their punishments, and even the Furies grow teary-eyed (10.40–8). As in Virgil's memorable account in the fourth *Georgic*, the rulers of Hades are moved to compassion and allow Orpheus to rescue Eurydice, but then he fails through love and breaks their conditions by looking back, thus losing her.

Seeking solitude on the Thracian hillside, he attracts with his music a virtual arboretum of trees that "crowd into a shade" (10.90–105), and wild creatures and birds sit attentively round him like an audience as he tunes his strings (143–4). Ovid gives Orpheus a formal proem, in which he invokes his mother, the Muse, and acknowledges tradition by proposing Jupiter as the proper opening theme but then excuses his substitution of a lighter program consisting of tales of boys loved by the gods and the sinful passions of girls. It is not his erotic material that will destroy Orpheus but his earlier denunciation of women, which leads to the brutal attack by the Thracian maenads, whose Bacchic cries and noisy instruments prevent them from hearing the melody of his lyre; if they had heard it, says Ovid, then surely the very stones they threw would have grown soft. Instead, the rocks (just now part of his attentive audience) grew red with the blood of the poet, whose appeal (this time) went unheard. When Orpheus is torn apart, his head and lyre are received by the river Hebrus and float, murmuring pitiable laments, down to the sea, while the poet's shade is reunited with his beloved wife in death.

Orpheus was needed here to complete Ovid's implied manifesto of art, which is also carried to its extreme form in one of Orpheus's tales. The requited love of Pygmalion will claim our attention again in the context of relations between the sexes, but it would be negligent to write about Ovid's presentation of the artist without including the story that attributes to art its most miraculous success. In Greek myth it was Daedalus who was famous for making statues seem to live and move, and one might ask why Ovid has excluded this aspect of Daedalus's artistry from the *Metamorphoses*, celebrating Daedalus only for his invention of wings, to escape from Crete, and the tragic death of his little son. Perhaps Ovid excluded Daedalus's achievements as a sculptor because they involve no metamorphosis, perhaps because he wanted no competition with his own romantic account of the artist and lover Pygmalion. Certainly, Ovid is conscious of Daedalus's pride as an inventor, which motivates his jealous killing of his nephew and apprentice, young Perdix (8.235–55). But what marks Daedalus out is his suffering as a father: like the sun god, he loses his child because the boy does not heed his anxious instructions, and he cannot save him. Here we can compare the poignant repetitions of Ovid's verse in Latin with the English version (which substitutes a third repetition of "where" for the third calling of his name):

> *At pater infelix nec iam pater "Icare" dixit*
> *"Icare" dixit, "ubi es? qua te regione requiram?"*
> *"Icare" dicebat: pennas adspexit in undis*
> *devovitque suas artes.*

> His wretched father, now no father, cried
> "Oh Icarus, where are you? Icarus,
> Where shall I look, where find you?" On the waves
> He saw the feathers. Then he cursed his skill. (8.231–4,
>   tr. Melville)

Pygmalion as Creator

We know from other writers that in the Cypriot myth Pygmalion was a king, not an artist, and was lustfully infatuated with a statue of the goddess Venus, which he took from the sanctuary and polluted with his embrace—a tyrant and a sinner whom the goddess would not wish to reward. It is Ovid who makes Pygmalion into a shy sculptor, alienated from living women by their assumed vulgarity and lechery. And it is in a spirit of humility that the sculptor shapes the most beautiful girl he can imagine:

> Meanwhile he carved his snow-white ivory
> With marvelous triumphant artistry
> And gave it perfect shape, more beautiful
> Than any woman born. His masterwork
> Fired him with love. It seemed to him alive,
> Its face to be a real girl's, a girl
> Who wished to move—but modesty forbade.
> Such art his art concealed. (10.247–52, tr. Melville)

In homage to her beauty he offers gifts and adorns her with jewelry, laying the image on a luxurious couch. When the feast of Venus approaches, he sacrifices and prays to the goddess for a wife like his ivory maiden (not daring to voice his real desire for the maiden herself). Venus sends a sign of her blessing, and on his return he kisses the statue and feels it grow warm and soft to his touch—as if she were a wax model taking shape beneath his fingers. As he caresses the image, it first becomes flesh, then responds to his kisses, looking on her creator and lover at the moment she sees the light of day. In this tale of wish fulfillment, they are married and she gives birth to a son, Paphos (10.280–97).

Women readers may feel less enthusiasm for this story of the perfect wife and its implied guarantee that she will never show discontent or independence. (Compare Michael Longley's poem in Hofmann and Lasdun, *The New Metamorphoses,* in which Pygmalion's passion melts his new bride to nothing.) But it is more important to ask to what extent or in what sense Ovid really believed an artist could give life. Ovid certainly had faith in the transcendence of the highest art. How far is this story a myth of artistic creation, and how far a simple miracle of piety rewarded? Is Pygmalion any more magically endowed than the pious Deucalion and Pyrrha? And is the final metamorphosis from ivory to living flesh really of a higher order than the initial metamorphosis from elephant tusk to a divine image like that of Athena Parthenos? Historically, ivory would be used only as an overlay for the exposed flesh of a life-size statue: it is already extraordinary for the sculptor to model a whole body in ivory. In Ovid's day life-size marble Aphrodites were more available in Rome, and I suspect he has made Pygmalion's maiden of ivory just because such elaborate work would be altogether beyond normal ambition. So, to my skeptical reading, this miracle is actually a less serious expression of Ovid's belief in the powers of art than the myths of poetry and music that both precede and follow it.

Further Reading

On Ovid's artists, see E. W. Leach, "*Ekphrasis* and the Theme of Artistic Failure in Ovid's *Metamorphoses*," *Ramus* 3 (1974): 102–42; D. Lateiner, "Mythic and Non-mythic Artists in Ovid's *Metamorphoses*," *Ramus* 13 (1984): 1–30. On weaving and the development of the Roman concept of text, see J. Scheid and J. Svenbro, *The Craft of Zeus,* tr. C. Volk (Cambridge, Mass., 1996), 131–7. See also C. P. Segal, "Philomela's Web and the Pleasures of the Text: Reader and Violence in the *Metamorphoses* of Ovid," in *Modern Critical Theory and Classical Literature,* ed. I. J. F. de Jong and J. P. Sullivan (Leiden, 1994), 257–80. On Pygmalion, see P. R. Hardie, *Ovid's Poetics of Illusion* (Cambridge, 2002); J. Elsner and A. Sharrock, "Reviewing Pygmalion," *Ramus* 20 (1991): 149–82; also A. Sharrock, "Womanufacture," *Journal of Roman Studies* 81 (1991): 36–49. On more general aspects of depicting transformation, see A. Sharrock, "Representing Metamorphosis," in *Art and Text in Roman Culture,* ed. J. Elsner (Cambridge, 1996), 103–30.

·5·

The Lives of Women

The Feminine Gender

We saw in chapter 3 that Teiresias had the unique experience of downward transformation from male to female and engineered his return to male status. Although he also reported to Jupiter and Juno that women had more pleasure than men from sexual intercourse, he clearly believed the privileges of masculinity outweighed these (unexplained) pleasures. Similarly, young Hermaphroditus clearly feels that he has been victimized by his transformation from male to epicene, that is, having sexual characteristics of both genders. In Ovid's time, as usually now, men enjoyed a superior status to women and believed it was their entitlement. In two other tales the metamorphosis is a sex change, one eagerly desired, from female to male, but the motives for desiring this change are completely different.

The story of Iphis (9.666–797) is determined first by socioeconomic and later by emotional need. A poor man, Ligdus, from Phaestos in Crete told his pregnant wife that he hoped she would have an easy delivery and bear him a son: since he could not afford to rear a daughter, a female child would have to be killed. This was not unusual in the ancient world, where fathers needed their sons' physical labor or earning skills and would have to pay a dowry in order to get their daughters married. Girl babies might be abandoned in the hope that some childless person or slave dealer would rear them. In romantic comedies a wife might secretly rear a girl if her husband was away from home, and this is what Telethousa did with her child, bringing her up as a boy and giving her the unisex name Iphis.

In the Greek version of this myth mother and daughter were saved from the father's anger by the intervention of Leto (Latona), but Ovid changes both the goddess and the story. First, it is Isis (protectress of women) who appears to Telethousa before the birth, promising her help in saving the expected baby girl. Second, Iphis actually reaches puberty and is betrothed by her father to her school friend Ianthe, with whom she is in love, as is Ianthe with her future "husband." Ovid gives to Iphis an extended soliloquy expressing, along with her fear of discovery, her deep distress at what she sees as an unnatural love. (Greek and Roman society did not accept lesbian relationships with the tolerance they displayed toward relations between man and boy.) Her mother desperately postpones the wedding until it is inevitable, then she and her daughter supplicate Isis for the promised help. The goddess fills the temple with happy omens, and as they leave, Iphis develops a longer stride, her features and body grow stronger, and her hair becomes shorter—in short, she has become a youth. Rejoicing, they dedicate gifts to Isis with the inscription "The boy Iphis has paid with gifts the vow he made as a woman." Then Venus, Juno, and Hymen, god of marriage, assemble to bless the union.

The other sex change has a more painful origin. Virgil had introduced among the women of the underworld Caenis, who became the warrior Caeneus, then returned in death to her original gender (*Aen.* 6.448). In Ovid's Trojan sequence Nestor compares the invincible warrior Cycnus, son of Neptune, with the warrior Caeneus (12.189–90). He explains that there was once a beautiful Thessalian girl, Caenis, who rejected all her suitors but was surprised alone on the seashore and raped by Neptune. When he offered her a wish, she answered that she was entitled to a great favor in return for a great wrong. She wanted never to experience rape again: "grant me not to be a woman!" And as she spoke her voice deepened (11.203−5), and the god gave her the added power of not being penetrable by any weapon: no steel could kill her. Later, in the extended brawl caused by drunken centaurs at the wedding feast of Pirithous, Caeneus performed valiant feats, killing five of them (12.459). Then a giant centaur, Latreus, insulted him as a former woman, telling him to leave war and go back to spinning. His spear and sword shattered against Caeneus's body, and Caeneus plunged his sword into his enemy. Even when all the centaurs converged upon Caeneus, they could not inflict any wounds until they buried him with uprooted tree trunks, crushing him into the ground. Nestor quotes two versions of the warrior's death: that he was finally forced down through the earth into Hades, or, as the prophet Mopsus declared, that he soared up to heaven as a bird (12.522−31). Mopsus's final tribute, "hail, once great glory of the Lapiths and now unique bird of your kind," may seem to avoid the anticlimactic return to feminine gender, but Ovid equivocates: in Latin birds are treated as feminine in gender.

The Ubiquity of Rape

Ovid has no doubt of the insult done to Caenis, but the sheer brevity of the account of her rape and of other reports where women are seen, lusted after, and possessed in a line of verse speaks for the commonness of such assaults. The poem began with Apollo's attempted rape of Daphne (saved by becoming an impenetrable tree) and continued with Jupiter's rape of Io, Pan's attempted rape of Syrinx, and Jupiter's rape of Callisto, who is cruelly rejected by Diana when her pregnancy becomes apparent. As Arachne's tapestry demonstrated, gods took what they wanted, and divine rapes were the origin of Perseus and many other heroes. One instance deserves a query in passing: the so-called rape of Proserpina in book 5. Dis certainly intends sexual rape but, as the story is told, it seems still possible for Demeter to regain her child after he has carried her down to Hades: the negotiations with Jupiter seem to imply that she is still a virgin, and the "marriage" is validated only by the fact that Proserpina has eaten the pomegranate seeds in the house of Dis. Rape language is far more explicit in the god's violation of the brave nymph Cyane, who tries to block his chariot's path: "urging on his dreadful team he buried his royal scepter, hurled by his powerful arm into the depths of her pool, and the stricken earth opened a path into Tartarus" (5.421–3). Cyane both is, and is not, her pool, and the inconsolable wound in her heart that melts her into weeping waters is perhaps only a metaphorical rape. Certainly, there are enough physical ones ahead of us. But after book 5 the rapes of mortals or nymphs will be by demigods, by natural forces like river deities or the North Wind, Boreas (6.702–10), by the centaur Nessus (9.108–33), or even by mortals. Only one case—the almost incidental double rape of Chione by Apollo and Mercury (11.303–10)—is inflicted by the usual gods.

Most of us hear and read more about rapes than we would wish, but sexual pursuit is so recurrent in *Metamorphoses* that Ovid's achievement of variety is an index of both his skill and his audience's taste. Let me illustrate from one frustrated rape, as experienced by the escaped victim, and one uniquely horrible narrative of rape and sexual abuse.

First, for one of the typical rapes and attempted rapes by a natural force, our informant is the nymph and huntress Arethusa, who (as readers of Ovid would see it) tempted providence by going bathing (5.572–641). She describes with leisured detail how she found clear waters that flowed without eddies, where willow and poplar provided shade and were themselves sheltered by sloping banks. Slipping off her clothes, she submerged herself naked in the waters and began to swim. Then she heard a voice from below the surface and climbed in terror on to the nearest bank. She describes how the river god Alpheus accosted her as she hesitated at the water's edge. "'Where are you hurrying, Arethusa?' he called in a hoarse voice out of his waters: 'Where are you hurrying?' I ran, naked as I was, for my clothes were on the other bank. This just made him more eager and panting: being naked made me seem easier to take. I kept running like this and the savage fellow kept closing in on me, as doves flee the hawk with trembling wing, and as the hawk pressed upon trembling doves" (5.599–606). In a long nightmare chase over a number of named Arcadian landmarks, she sees his shadow looming (Alpheus is still to be imagined as a man) and hears his footsteps; in despair she begs Diana for rescue and is enveloped by the goddess in a cloud. But Alpheus circles around questing for her. Now she feels the terror of lambs in the sheepfold as the wolf howls outside, and suddenly she finds herself melting until she becomes a stream. But this lays her open to his other, watery form. Guessing her identity he turns himself into his own stream to unite with her. In this crisis Diana cleaves open the ground for Arethusa to submerge into underground caverns and reach Ortygia, the island site of Syracuse, where her spring emerges again into the daylight (and can still be seen, spouting fresh water only a few feet from the sea).

The dual nature of the river god gives a surreal intensity to the chase, in which even Arethusa's divine protectress has to intervene twice, finally sending her belowground in a rescue curiously antithetical to the rape undergone by the other water spirit, Cyane. The victim's narrative commands attention both by its vivid description of landscape and by its constant change of natural medium.

The first—and only—rape by a human comes in the transition from divine vengeance to the evils that humans inflict on each other—*homo homini lupus* (man on man like a wolf)—in book 6. Ovid combines the worst crimes in the dreadful tale of incest, murder, and cannibalism which starts when the barbarian king Tereus of Thrace rapes the sister of his wife, the Athenian princess Procne (6.424–674). Their story had been made into a tragedy by Sophocles; though this play is lost, a surviving excerpt conveys the anxieties of the new bride—of any bride—taken from her home to live among foreigners and alien gods. Tereus, at first loving, returns to Athens at his wife's request to fetch her beloved sister Philomela for a visit. But once he sees her he is possessed by lust. Her family have entrusted her to him, but once he has her in Thrace Tereus drags her into the deep forest and takes the defenseless virgin by force as she cries out, weeping and trembling and appealing in vain to the gods. As with Daphne, Ovid applies the imagery of predator and prey to Tereus, who is like an eagle with a hare (516–7), and to Philomela, who trembles like a wounded lamb shaken from the wolf's jaws or a dove dreading the eagle (6.527–30). When she finds her voice, she curses him for destroying all the bonds of family and threatens to denounce him to man and nature. He draws his sword and grabs her by her hair to strike, but instead of killing her,

> he seized
> Her tongue with tongs and with his brutal sword
> Cut it away. The root jerked to and fro;
> The tongue lay on the dark soil muttering
> And wriggling, as the tail cut off a snake
> Wriggles, and as it died, it tried to reach
> Its mistress' feet. Even after that dire deed
> Men say (could I believe it), lusting still,
> Oft on the poor maimed girl he wreaked his will.
>   (6.556–62, tr. Melville)

There is no more gruesome picture in Ovid's entire work, unless perhaps it is the terrible moment still to come when Procne, in revulsion and vengeance on Tereus, embraces and slays her little son, like a tigress slaying a young deer (624–42).

In one sense, however, the story of Procne's revenge is a beginning. Unless we count the demented Agave, she is the first woman in Ovid's narrative to plan and commit murder, and the first of a series of women to dare criminal acts. This euphemism must stretch to cover the sequence of virgins driven to action by love from the young Medea in book 7 to Scylla in book 8 to the incestuous urges of Byblis in book 9 and the incest of Myrrha consummated in book 10. But it will be better to postpone these dangerous lovers until the next chapter.

Becoming a Mother

In real life and in Ovid's epic women's lives continue beyond their sexual flowering, past rape, seduction, or marriage to conception, childbirth, motherhood, and, in tragic cases, the premature loss of beloved children. Ovid devotes more concern than most poets to the mother and child during gestation and labor (see, e.g., 7.125–7; 10.510–4; 15.216–21). We saw how Semele's pregnancy by Jupiter provoked the cruel hatred of Juno and led to the miraculous incubation of her posthumous child, Dionysus, in Jupiter's thigh. Juno was no less jealous of Latona, whom she drove across the Aegean in a desperate quest for a place to give birth. In book 6, an old Lycian connects a mysterious altar in a marsh with the story of Latona's flight from Juno (6.332–81). The floating island of Delos consented to stay still while she gave birth to the twins Apollo and Diana beneath a palm tree, but Juno drove her on and she came, carrying her twins, to Lycia. Because she was parched with thirst and the eager twins had drained her milk, she begged the reed gatherers to let her drink at their lake but they refused. Although she supplicated them, promising gratitude, they abused her and deliberately muddied the waters. So Latona cursed them to perpetual life as amphibians and they became frogs.

It is again Juno who tries to obstruct Alcmene when she is in labor with Hercules. In the Greek version she persuaded the Fates to watch the woman in labor with crossed arms to inhibit birth, but they were tricked by a loyal servant girl, Galinthias, who told them Alcmene had delivered her child, so that they relaxed their arms and Hercules could come to birth. The Romans revered Juno herself as "Lucina," goddess of childbirth, so she needed no help from the Fates. Many of Ovid's most vivid narratives are told by their subjects: Alcmene herself recalls (9.281–323) how she was straining in labor and called on Lucina for help. But Juno had seated herself on the altar by the house door, out of sight, pressing her left leg under her right knee and holding her crossed arms with fingers interlaced, muttering spells to block the birth. When Galanthis (as Ovid names her) saw Juno outside, she addressed her, "Whoever you are, congratulate my mistress, who is delivered and has her wish." Juno is deceived, but when the maid laughs at her trick, the goddess turns her into a weasel, the domestic beast which supposedly gave birth through its mouth. The story is told in an intimate moment between Alcmene and her daughter-in-law Iole, as they adjust to the news of Hercules' final apotheosis. Ovid seems to know the world of women in the family, and not just the world of pretty and promiscuous girls.

But Iole too has a tale of metamorphosis: the fate of her sister Dryope. Here too the pathos of the story has been created by Ovid's changes. In the version of her transformation reported from Nicander, Dryope was raped by Apollo and gave birth to a boy, Amphissos. When Amphissos was an adult, he dedicated a temple to the nymphs, and when Dryope went to worship at the temple, she was changed into a nymph, and a mysterious poplar tree grew up beside her—or perhaps by her pool. But Ovid starts after the rape, with Dryope now a happy mother and wife of Andraemon (9.328–93). Iole herself went with Dryope and her child, still suckling at the breast, to gather garlands for the nymphs by the lake. As Dryope picked lotus branches to give her son, Iole saw blood ooze out. Here Ovid has grafted another metamorphosis. This lotus plant was actually the nymph Lotis, transformed to save her from Priapus's lust (but Priapus is frustrated in the version of Ovid's *Fasti*). Although Dryope recoiled in distress at the bloodshed, she began to take root, and bark rose up to cramp her limbs; even her arms became branches, and the milk dried up in her breasts. Neither Iole nor Andraemon could prevent it, and soon only her face remained human. As with dying farewells in opera, the length (twenty-one lines) of Dryope's last speech slightly detracts from the pathos of her obliteration, as does her identification with the tree she is becoming. First, she protests her innocence of any malice: if she is lying, then may she lose her leaves and be hacked by axes! She begs her husband to protect her from scythes and nibbling sheep, but her last words ask them to stand on tiptoe to embrace her and lift up her son for a farewell kiss; then they should no longer resist but let the bark cover her eyes and mouth.

Ovid was surely writing for a female audience and shrewdly allowed the touch of comedy to dilute the otherwise painful narrative. Too many young mothers died in childbirth for an episode like this to be without emotional resonances. And the same risk of provoking real sorrow lurked behind the last of the four themes I have selected for this chapter: the grief of mothers at the deaths of their warrior sons and more helpless daughters.

The Mother Bereaved

In Ovid's Rome, as in classical Greece, it was the mother's role to close the eyes of the family dead and lay out the body. Once it left the house the duties of cremation or burial were taken over by the son or male next of kin. It was seen as normal for the younger generation to bury their parents, and tragic for the parent to have to bury the child, but warfare made this reversal of natural order only too common. A death became more tragic if in some way the family was prevented from completing the ritual for the dead, and this is the key to several of the scenes in which Ovid dwells on the bereaved mother's sorrow. Thus, when Phaethon is struck by the thunderbolt, Clymene does not know where to find him but scours the world in order to bury his body. When she (with his sisters) reaches the scene of his death, the nymphs have already buried him and inscribed his epitaph, so Clymene is reduced to embracing his name on the cold tomb. His sisters prolong their mourning for so many months that they are transformed into weeping poplars (2.340–66); a similar transformation turns the weeping sisters of dead Meleager into birds (8.533–46).

But the prototype of the mourning mother was Niobe, wife of Amphion, king of Thebes. In the last book of the *Iliad*, when Priam comes to beg Achilles to ransom the corpse of Hector, Achilles asks Priam to eat with him, "for even Niobe buried her children and put an end to her mourning" (24.602–17). Ovid does not change the Homeric outline but adds local color and intensifies Niobe's offense. While she herself is the epitome of arrogance, her children's fate exemplifies the ruthlessness of gods ready to destroy innocent lives in their revenge upon an offender (as Euripides' Aphrodite destroyed Phaedra for revenge on Hippolytus, who would not worship her). After Pallas Athene's punishment of Arachne (see ch. 4), Niobe's punishment by Apollo and Diana for insulting their mother, Latona (6.148–312), will be followed by Latona's punitive transformation of the Lycian peasants into frogs (6.316–81) and Apollo's flaying of the rival musician, the satyr Marsyas (382–400; see ch. 4).

Ovid may have modeled his treatment on Sophocles' tragedy, known to us only from a damaged papyrus of the *hypothesis* (plot outline) and vivid fragments of dialogue and chorus. We saw in chapter 3 that Ovid's epic version of the death of Pentheus avoided the terrible last moments of Euripides' *Bacchae* when Agave comes to herself and realizes she has dismembered and killed her own son. Like Pentheus, Niobe refuses reverence to the goddess Latona and her children, Apollo and Diana, when other Thebans welcome them. With insufferable arrogance Niobe demands to be worshiped instead because of her royal birth and marriage, her beauty, and especially her fertility as the mother of seven sons and seven daughters, whereas Latona has only the twins. Upset by the possible loss of worship, Latona complains to her children, who promise her instant action. They fly unseen to Thebes, where the seven sons are riding and exercising outside the citadel (in Sophocles they were hunting). Each in turn is shot by unseen arrows, each, as Ovid describes them, with a different wound, even while they are trying to help their siblings.

Sophocles had represented Amphion as killed by Apollo when he tried to fight back in defense of his sons, but Ovid's Amphion kills himself in despair. This increases the contrast between husband and wife, as Niobe only becomes more arrogant and boasts that she still has more children than Latona (280–5). Now her daughters gather lamenting around the funeral biers of their brothers. A particularly grim fragment of Sophocles seems to be spoken by Apollo to Artemis (Diana), directing her aim: "do you see that frightened girl inside, cowering alone, trying to hide by the bins in the storeroom? Why not aim a swift arrow at her before she can escape in hiding?" (frag. 441a). Again Ovid diverges, switching from the more detailed account of the young men's deaths to dispatch the girls with frightening speed (ten lines, where the sons' deaths had required fifty!), until only one is left, whom Niobe tries to shelter with her body, uttering a desperate appeal. As she sits

> Amid her sons, her daughters, and her husband,
> All lifeless corpses, rigid in her ruin,
> Her hair no breeze can stir; her cheeks are drained
> And bloodless; in her doleful face her eyes
> Stare fixed and hard—a likeness without life. (6.301–5,
>   tr. Melville)

Niobe's transformation—which the tragedy could only have encompassed through the prophecy of a deus ex machina—completes itself as her tongue and all her limbs stiffen, until her very flesh (and we should think here of her reproductive womb) is stone, yet she still weeps. There was a legend that Mount Sipylus in Niobe's native Phrygia was the petrified queen mother. Ovid boldly has the winds transport her home, where she is absorbed into the mountain peak whose streams are her ever-flowing tears.

Ovid must also include more complex tales of mothers like Procne, who kills her son by the rapist Tereus, or Althaea, who is driven by vengeance for her brothers to murder her own son, in retaliation for his killing them: such terrible conflicting emotions can only be resolved by suicide or metamorphosis. But he develops most fully the mourning of Hecuba, celebrated in the Euripidean tragedy named after her. In fact, her bereavements form the climax of Ovid's fall of Troy. Her tragedy begins after the deaths of Hector and his killer Achilles, when Priam too has been slain at the household altar, and Hector's son Astyanax has been thrown from the battlements of Troy. Only the women are left, and the youngest son Polydorus, who had been sent away for safety to King Polymestor of Thrace (13.429–38). Captured princesses, like all other women prisoners, were allotted as slaves to the Greek chieftains, but Polyxena, Hecuba's only surviving daughter, is demanded as a sacrifice by a ghost, the dead Achilles. Echoing Euripides, Ovid reports (13.449–80) the nobility of young Polyxena, who refuses to be handled and dies freely with a spirit worthy of a princess. But he has streamlined the tragic sequence so as to subordinate even this human sacrifice to the grief of Hecuba, whose passionate speech devotes more attention to her own death in life as Ulysses' captive than to grieving for her daughter, who has won liberty in death (13.494–532).

Now a second loss overwhelms the bereaved mother. As she fetches water from the shore to wash her daughter's body, she finds the floating corpse of her youngest son, bearing Polymestor's murderous wounds. Here Ovid remodels Euripides' dramatic form to narrate Hecuba's emotional transformation from grief to bitter vengeance. Now she is as silent as Niobe, and her *dolor* (both grief and anger) consumes her tears; she freezes like a rock as she gazes for a second time at her dead child and then "arms herself with anger" (13.544). Revitalized, Hecuba carries out a deceitful revenge on the treacherous king, urging the other women captives to surround him as she gouges out his eyes. Finally, as she is stoned by the king's Thracian people in their fury, a physical metamorphosis follows the more important psychological transformation. It was an old tradition that Hecuba had been changed into a bitch because of her rabid cursing, and Euripides presents this in prophetic form at the end of his play (as he had the metamorphosis of Cadmus and Harmonia into serpents). Ovid's narrative incorporates the change and invokes the promontory of Cynossema (Dog's Tomb) as a monument to her howls of grief over the Thracian wilderness.

But the poet cannot leave Troy without restoring a less despairing mood, which he achieves by moving back to an earlier time, when the goddess Aurora mourned her son Memnon, killed in combat by Achilles long before the fall of Troy. Aurora's grief is altogether more self-centered, as she petitions Jupiter for some honor to her dead son to compensate for what she sees as neglect of her worship and ingratitude for her daily services to gods and men.

Jupiter assents, and as Memnon's body burns on the pyre, smoke begins to swirl, like mists arising from a river, and becomes a flock of birds, who take on military formations and fight a ritual combat over his tomb (13.576–619). Ovid has made only small changes to this Greek tale, but one is to call the birds Memnon's sisters, echoing the ritual role of mourning played by sisters (like the sisters of Phaethon and Meleager), and to assimilate the birds' annual migration and return to the Roman rite of *parentalia* on the anniversary of a kinsman's death. The tale also permits him to return to the present, with the morning dew that each day witnesses Aurora's continuing tears.

In singling out Ovid's representation of these phases in a woman's life, I have not, of course, meant to imply that the emotion of love, whether mutual or unrequited, is not also central to the lives of women. But this theme is too important, and Ovid's portrayal of love is itself too varied, to be confined within this survey. Let love, then, be the unifying theme of the tales considered in the next chapter.

Further Reading

Amy Richlin, "Reading Ovid's Rapes," in *Pornography and Representation in Greece and Rome*, ed. Amy Richlin (New York, 1992, 158–79); Genevieve Lively, "Reading Resistance in Ovid's *Metamorphoses*," in *Ovidian Transformations: Essays on Ovid's "Metamorphoses" and Its Reception*, ed. Philip R. Hardie, Alessandro Barchiesi, and Stephen Hinds (Cambridge, 1999), 197–213; A. Keith, *Engendering Rome: Women in Latin Epic* (Cambridge, 2000), chs. 3–4.

·6·

Aspects of Love

Some critics have argued that love is the real theme of Ovid's great poem, and there can be no doubt that what Brooks Otis (1970) called "the pathos of love" is the heart of the central section of *Metamorphoses*, from the Tereus episode in book 6 to the end of book 11. By the end of book 6, however, the poet has only added one particularly cruel human counterpart to the earlier divine rapes. With the story of Medea that opens book 7, Ovid introduces his first love-struck girl and uses her confused response to this new emotion as a model for what will be a series of women in love. But by referring to "the story of Medea" I am begging the question. This seventh book follows Jason and the other Greek heroes to barbaric Colchis in his quest for the golden fleece, which is the talisman ensuring the prosperity of King Aeetes' land. In Colchis, Aeetes sets Jason the terrible tasks of yoking fire-breathing bulls to plow the earth with dragon's teeth. All this was familiar to Ovid's readers: they would know from Apollonius's *Voyage of the Argonauts*, or its Latin adaptation by Varro of Atax, how Jason succeeded with the help of Aeetes' young daughter, so smitten with love that she fled with the Greek stranger and even murdered her brother on the dangerous return voyage to Greece. They would be even more familiar with the tragic outcome of this adventure, in the version first shaped by Euripides. In this tragedy Jason abandoned Medea to marry a Greek princess. Threatened with exile, Medea destroyed the bride and killed both their sons, expressing in an extended soliloquy the torment of this decision. Euripides' play was closely adapted by Ennius early in the second century, and Ovid himself had composed both a dramatized monologue in the form of a letter to Jason (*Heroides* [Letters from heroines] 12) and a tragedy about Medea's terrible vengeance.

The Medea who falls in love with Jason in *Metamorphoses* 7 is altogether different: for her Ovid composes a soliloquy of sixty lines to reflect the struggle between reason and passion in her heart. She does not understand her emotional confusion; can this be what is called loving? Why is she so anxious for the handsome stranger? "My reason urges me one way, my desire another; I see the better course of action, but I am following the worse" (7.20–21). Her love for this stranger is unauthorized and entails a betrayal of her country. To this extent, Medea foreshadows the unlawful passions of Scylla, who kills her own father to win the love of Minos, her country's enemy; of Byblis, who suffers an impossible desire for her brother; and of Myrrha, who actually has a child by her own father. Much of Medea's stream of consciousness is peculiar to her situation. First is Jason's immediate ordeal—how can she watch him die? Ovid follows her daydreaming vision of binding him to marry her and take her to Greece, where she will be glorified by the married women as savior of the Greek heroes, and lets her speculate about the famous hazards of the clashing rocks that will beset their journey.

Even though Ovid's narrative will concentrate on Medea's exercise of magic to save Jason's father and destroy his enemy Pelias, readers of this first monologue will feel the dramatic irony generated between her expectations and the future tragedy. But what this monologue has in common with its successors is the Euripidean battle of conflicting purposes, as the imagined future triggers a renewal of wishful thinking and desire. Repeatedly, the voice of reason addresses Medea in the second person (17–8, 21–4, 69–71), and the narrative reports that duty and chastity have triumphed—until she happens to meet Jason alone in the precinct of Hecate. Then love takes control and duty is forgotten.

Perhaps the variety of both love itself and Ovid's narrative presentation are best illustrated by the story of Orpheus and the lays which Orpheus himself tells in book 10. Orpheus, originally the model poet and singer, had become the model of a tragic lover in Virgil's rewriting of his journey to the underworld. Before Virgil the myth had celebrated his successful recovery of his bride. But the fame of Virgil's account in the fourth *Georgic* both imposed the same tragic outcome on the loving couple and challenged Ovid to offer a different emotional tonality. So the relatively short narrative that opens *Metamorphoses* 10 imports an element of calculation into his journey "after he had lamented Eurydice enough to the upper air" and into his rhetorically plausible appeal to the rulers of Hades: even Orpheus's prolonged mourning, first outside the gates of Hades, then after he had fasted for a week on the slopes of Rhodope, is somehow discolored by his concern first with rejecting female suitors, then with recommending the love of boys as more satisfying because of their freshness in the springtime of life before manhood sets in (10.72–80).

Tragic Tales of Divine Love for Boys

These details are purposeful, and the entire construction of this book is ingenious. As Orpheus sings on the mountain he needs shade, and a forest of trees comes to screen him from the sun. He has just suffered a double bereavement: the tragic accident of his bride's death by snake bite and the second loss of Eurydice in Hades, which is his own fault. Although Orpheus will announce a formal program of singing about the love of gods for boys, before he tunes his lyre Ovid himself narrates one tale of a boy beloved by Apollo. The grief of Apollo's beloved Cyparissus after he has accidentally struck his pet stag is one of three tales of tragic accident reported in book 10, but the other two accidental deaths are part of Orpheus's double program, for he also announces a second theme, the unlawful loves of human girls. Orpheus's stories of Venus's rewards to those who love well also relate her punishments for abusing love, as in the tale that Orpheus composes for Venus to justify first her reward, then her punishment, of Atalanta and her lover, Hippomenes. The scale of the different tales increases from the short narratives of the first phase (up to the happy marriage that rewards Pygmalion and his statue-girl) to the extended miniature epic of Myrrha (10.298–502) and to the last lay, in which the tragic death of Venus's beloved Adonis is expanded by Venus's complex cautionary tale.

If we compare the apparently similar tragedy of Apollo's beloved Cyparissus, told by Ovid, with Orpheus's telling of the death of Hyacinthus, Apollo's other beloved boy, it is clear how the poet has exploited the similarities and differences between these two tales. The Cyparissus tale is offered to explain the origin of the cypress tree and mentions the love of the lyre-playing Apollo chiefly as a preliminary to the sad tale of Cyparissus's pet: the boy's devotion to his tame stag (modeled on the pet stag of Silvia mistakenly killed in *Aeneid* 7) parallels the god's love for the boy. It is the boy who accidentally wounds his own pet, and the god is affected only because the grieving boy asks the gods to let him mourn forever: as he mourns his hair grows shaggy, his limbs grow rough with bark, and his arms become outstretched branches. Grieving in his turn, the god has conferred on his beloved the honor of becoming the tree of mourning that comforts the bereaved.

Within Orpheus's song sequence, the untroubled love of Jupiter for Ganymede, raised to the skies to become divine cupbearer (10.155–61), precedes Apollo's second loss. (Orpheus has returned the theme to the loves of gods, and Venus will follow.) Orpheus begins by addressing Hyacinthus in his new form as flower. "Whenever spring drives off winter . . . you grow with your flowers from the green turf. It is you whom my father loved above all others; for you, Delphi at the earth's center lacked its presiding god while Apollo stayed by the Eurotas and unwalled Sparta. He paid no honor to his lyre nor his archery" (10.164–70). Then he returns to narrative: the boy was tragically killed while running to catch the discus thrown by the god. After desperately trying to bring him back to life, Apollo uttered the lament that Orpheus reproduces, ending with the promise that a new flower would imitate in writing his cries of grief, which would gain a second meaning in honoring a hero. Here the poet cleverly alludes to the letters AIAI, supposedly inscribed on the hyacinth's petals, and to the death of Ajax (AIAS), which Ovid will narrate in book 13. To Apollo's memorial flower Ovid adds the commemoration of the Spartans in an annual festival, the Hyacinthia, which "endure[s] to this very age" (10.217–8). We might compare this brief reminder of Ovid's own time with the less specific promise of Venus to dead Adonis that "the memory of my grief for you will persist for ever. Each year the representation of your death will reenact my mourning." Both stories are *aitia* (tales of origin), which gain solemnity from the continued rituals of commemoration.

The Wicked Passion of Girls

Two short tales of how Venus punished human evil link the guest-slaying Cerastae with the more relevant Propoetides, women who abused their beauty or shape (the key word *forma* becomes more prominent in these tales) in prostitution and were turned to stone. It was supposedly loathing of such women that led Pygmalion (in a counterpart of Orpheus's own loathing) to create his ideal woman of ivory and earn from Venus the reward of her animation into a live woman and the happy man's wife.

At this point the poet has to negotiate a violent change of mood from good love to its evil form, from innocent happiness to the deepest guilt. It takes a complex second proem to prepare the tone for the dreadful tale of Myrrha, the daughter of Pygmalion's grandson Cinyras. Orpheus opens in the tones of a priest and prophet, first with an oracular utterance "Cinyras could have been thought happy, if he had never had a daughter," then a solemn warning to daughters and fathers to shun his tale, but he undercuts his ban by adding that if they must hear it, they should not believe it ever happened or, failing that, believe that it was punished (10.298–303). This is one of those terrible tales that happen in foreign parts, and Orpheus congratulates the land of Thrace (where he himself will shortly be lynched by maenads) for being far from the spice-bearing lands where that tree, the myrrh bush, grows. We are, then, about to read the origin of another tree.

From myrrh Ovid cuts to Myrrha, whose passion can only have been induced by a Fury; Cupid denies all responsibility. This girl had many suitors but loved only one man—the worst of choices. After twenty lines, Orpheus has still not named her sinful passion. But Ovid and his readers knew the story from the celebrated miniature epic of Catullus's friend Cinna; its title was *Zmyrna,* another form of Myrrha's name. Orpheus leads from the girl's agonized soliloquy (10.320–55) to her conviction that her desire is inspired by the Furies and her decision to hang herself. But she is interrupted by her faithful nurse, from whom she tries in vain to conceal her incestuous love. For their dialogue and the nurse's wicked undertaking to arrange an assignation in disguise, Ovid has borrowed from the notorious scene in Euripides' *Hippolytus* in which Phaedra's nurse propositions her chaste stepson and destroys Phaedra's honor. Another premonitory sequence shows the moon and stars leaving the darkened sky in revulsion as the disguised girl is taken to her father's bed (446–64) and conceives from this first incestuous union. But as with the lustful Tereus, once is not enough, and she returns again and again until Cinyras finds a light and discovers the identity of his bedmate. He draws his sword to kill her but she escapes and wanders distraught in the wilderness, begging the gods to let her die in such a way that she will pollute neither the living nor the dead. Only metamorphosis can resolve this dilemma, and Myrrha feels her legs covered in earth and her feet taking root. Her torso becomes a long trunk in which the blood turns to sap, and her arms become branches. As the tree engulfs her growing womb, she buries her face in its bark, welcoming transformation—the very opposite of the feelings of poor Dryope (see ch. 5). Myrrha has lost human perceptions but her tears ooze from the bark and are honored by men with the girl's own name.

This is a harrowing tale, but the baby is still unborn. Always insisting on the new identity of the tree (10.495, 500, 505, 509, 512), Orpheus tells how it had no voice to cry out in labor pain to Lucina, but Lucina (in contrast with her appalling treatment of Alcmene) gently reaches out to the laboring tree and utters the words that induce birth. The tree splits and drops its burden on the ground: the baby wails healthily and becomes a beautiful child whom even Envy would praise, as lovely as naked Cupid himself.

Once again the key word *forma* (529) stresses the beauty of this growing adolescent as he approaches manhood, growing most handsome (*formosissimus* 522), even more handsome than himself (*se formosior ipso*), that is, than he was already. The transition converts the child born of a girl's unlawful love into the boy beloved of a god (the first category in Orpheus's program), but this time it is a female god, Venus herself, accidentally grazed by Cupid's erotogenic arrows as he kissed his mother.

Venus and Adonis

Orpheus describes Adonis (or Tammuz) as a man, but Venus's relationship with him is more like that of a mother, and his behavior that of a rash boy. In the last lay of book 10, Venus and Adonis hunt small game together and she begs him not to hunt dangerous beasts like lions or boars for fear that they will kill him. Since Adonis was killed by a boar, Ovid's readers may well have wondered at Venus's allusion to the anger and power of lions and her own hatred of the species. It is the cue for a story. Leading Adonis over to a pleasant shade, Venus lies with her head in his lap, interrupting her story to kiss the boy. The atmosphere has become quite cloying, but Orpheus's language betrays no emotional reaction to the goddess or her tale.

It begins with the girl athlete Atalanta, who could outrun all men. She had once consulted a god (unnamed) and been given the sinister oracle: "shun marriage; but you will not escape it and will be deprived of your identity while you still live" (10.566–7). So she devises a footrace to eliminate her suitors. If they want to marry her, they must outrun her; but if she wins, they must die. The hunter Hippomenes deplores the risk, but as he watches the contest and sees her face and body stripped for speed, he is overwhelmed with love. Venus narrates in character, dwelling lovingly on the power of Atalanta's beauty (*forma* again) to compel suitors, and her glorious body, "like mine, or even yours, if you became a woman" (579). Now Hippomenes risks his life by challenging her, and she in turn becomes enamored of the handsome athlete and devotes a soliloquy to him (10.611–35): "what god hates the handsome [*formosis*] and wants to destroy this man, forcing him to risk his life for marriage with me? I am not worth it" (a phrase Marsyas has already used for his discovery of the flute [6.386] and Orpheus for myrrh [10.310]). In her innocence, Atalanta, like young Medea, loves and does not realize this feeling is love (10.687). When Hippomenes turns to Venus for help, she provides him with three magic apples from a special sacred tree in Cyprus, to help him distract and overtake Atalanta. Since the myth of their race was familiar, Ovid/Orpheus gives Venus the expertise of a running commentator—but one who herself intervenes, forcing Atalanta to stoop for the last apple.

But this is a tale of ingratitude: Venus had rewarded Hippomenes' devotion before the race but now he did not even present to her a minimal offering of incense. The goddess describes her anger and its effect on the lovers, who in their mutual lust enter the shrine of Cybele and pollute it with intercourse. Cybele's image turns its gaze away and the mother goddess, after considering plunging them into the underworld, decides it is too small a penalty. She turns them into lions, which roar with anger, terrifying other animals, but are subjected to the yoke and pull her chariot (19.695–707).

Venus has demonstrated the consequences of disregarding her godhead; now she comes to the moral of her story, to warn Adonis against provoking big game. But it is useless. As soon as she has mounted her chariot and departed, he provokes a fatal hunting accident. He hurls his javelin at a wild boar, which is enraged by the glancing wound and gashes his thigh. As he groans in dying pain, Venus hears and returns, consoling him with the promise of perpetual imitation of her mourning. This was the festival of Adonia, celebrated with women's laments over the Mediterranean world and a more famous counterpart to the Hyacinthia, the mention of which ended Orpheus's group of boy deaths. To prepare for his metamorphosis, Venus invokes the precedent of Persephone, who turned her attendants into the mint plant to vindicate her right to transform Cinyras's heroic descendant. (Ovid/Orpheus is reminding his public of the connection between the middle and the final lay.) As she sprinkles Adonis's blood with nectar, a scarlet anemone springs up; but it is short-lived and shattered by the same winds from which it takes its name. This "dying fall" brings together both the short lives of these rash boys and the cult practice of planting shallow gardens of quick-growing flowers for the Adonia, which bloomed and died in a few days. Orpheus does not impose his own closure to this epilogue but falls silent. The next book will bring his death at the hands of the women he has rejected. Does Ovid consider it as his punishment for denouncing heterosexual love? Wisely he avoids any hint of moralizing over the poet's tragic end.

The Sorrows and Consolations of Mutual Married Love

After Orpheus's savage fate, the tone of book 11 soon changes: more than half of the narrative is occupied by the love story of Ceyx and Alcyone. So now let us consider Ovid's stories of true married love. The simple piety of Deucalion and Pyrrha is reproduced in affectionate detail in book 8, and then another narrator, Lelex, describes the hospitality shown by the old couple Baucis and Philemon toward the disguised Jupiter and Mercury. Asked by the grateful gods to name their wish, Philemon asks only that they may live and die together: "Grant that the selfsame hour may take us both, / That I my consort's tomb may never see, / Nor may it fall to her to bury me" (8.709–10). This wish is fulfilled when, after serving the new shrine of the gods, they are ready for death and are transformed into two trees growing from a common trunk (8.720).

Such union in death and transfiguration is denied to the tormented love of Cephalus and Procris but will be the consummation of the tragedy of Ceyx and Alcyone. Each story helps to cast light on the distinctive qualities of the other.

It is Cephalus himself who narrates the tragedy of his marriage, an aging Cephalus who has come as envoy from Athens to ask the help of Aeacus and his sons against the threatened attack of Minos, king of Crete. Aeacus agrees and sends Telamon and Peleus to organize his supporting force, leaving his youngest son, Phocus (Ovid will report his murder incidentally in 11.267), to entertain his guest. When Phocus asks Cephalus about the curious hunting spear that he is carrying, one of his companions confirms that it has magical powers, homing in on whatever the hunter aims at and returning after it has hit its prey. But Cephalus himself is pained by the question, which recalls the tragic loss of his wife. He answers with a flood of memories, but, as Ovid indicates, he is both revealing and suppressing the truth of his marriage. He declares bitterly that the hunting spear destroyed him as it did his wife. But although he stresses his love for Procris throughout his narrative (7.690–862), theirs was a troubled and jealous relationship. Only a month after their wedding, while out hunting alone, he was seized by the dawn goddess, Aurora, who kept him against his will until she was persuaded by his longing for Procris to let him go. But he acted on her suggestion and returned home in disguise, to test his wife's fidelity. Finding her faithful and grieving for her lost husband, the false suitor persisted until she yielded, and then revealed himself, covering her with reproaches. In anger Procris left him and sought isolation from men in the mountains, hunting with Diana. Only when Cephalus begged her to forgive him did she return to him, and the hunting spear (a gift from Diana) was the gift of Procris to him on their reconciliation, along with a marvelous hound that always caught its prey. (Mention of the hound leads Cephalus to digress, explaining how he had used the hound to track a fierce fox that was ravaging Thebes. Since the fox was supernaturally immune to being caught, the gods had resolved the logical dilemma of this chase by turning both hound and prey to stone.)

Phocus persists (794–5): how did the hunting spear cause Cephalus so much grief? It seems Cephalus had learnt nothing from his early experiences and, despite his great happiness with Procris, persisted in going out alone to hunt. As he explains it, he loved to enjoy the breezes when he rested after his exertions and would call on Aura (Breeze) to enfold him and bring him repose. A meddlesome informer told Procris that her husband was engaging in a liaison, and she was tormented into suspicion. To paraphrase Cephalus's account, "when the next light of Dawn [*aurora*] drove away the night, I went out to hunt and Procris followed me into the wild, and as I called, as usual, for Aura to refresh me, Procris rushed out of the thickets. I thought it was a game animal, and discharged my unerring spear, which gave her a fatal wound. But her cries showed me my terrible mistake." He rushed to bind her wound and cradled her in his arms, and quotes her last words: "by the bonds of our marriage, and by the gods . . . by whatever I did for you, and our enduring love which caused my death, do not accept Aura into our bed" (7.852–6). It was small comfort that he was able to convince her of his love before she breathed her last.

This complicated tale of misadventures is in fact less complex than the Greek myths associated with Cephalus and Procris, which Ovid had refined. Ovid's Procris is innocent of yielding to persistent seduction in her husband's absence. Indeed, Ovid's first version of her story was introduced in the third book of the *Art of Love* in order to warn women against unwarranted suspicion of their lovers, using her accidental death as an example. But Nicander and other Greek writers recorded further infidelities and jealousies on both sides. In one version, Cephalus had stayed away from his bride for eight years to test her, before returning in disguise at the malicious suggestion of Aurora. In another, Procris had fled to King Minos of Crete, become his mistress, and cured him of a loathsome sexual disease, in return for which Minos, not Diana, gave her the magic spear. She then disguised herself as a young man, made friends with Cephalus, and offered him the spear in return for allowing homosexual penetration. (Since Cephalus has the spear, we must assume he consented.) There are traces of a shameful origin to the spear at line 587 when Ovid introduces Cephalus's speech—"he keeps silent on the price he paid for it"—but the line has been suspected by scrupulous editors. Instead, it seems Ovid has inscribed Cephalus's infidelity through the punning affinity between Aurora and Aura (impossible in Greek) and even the conventional epic use of Aurora's name quoted above ("next light of dawn"). Yet no one can deny Cephalus's belief that he loved Procris, reiterated eight times during his embarrassed tale.

In comparison, the mutual love of Ceyx and Alcyone is as innocent as it is intense. This is the achievement of Ovid himself, who eliminated a less sympathetic Greek narrative in which the gods drowned Ceyx to punish him and his wife, either for calling themselves Zeus and Hera or for boasting that they were the equals of the divine couple. Not only did Ovid eliminate any blame from their story, but he enriched it with a wealth of grandiose natural phenomena, new elements of the marvelous, and speeches that expressed the loving woman's perspective. But Ovid has also taken pains to link the two stories of married love. He introduces Ceyx, king of Trachis, when Peleus comes to him for purification after killing his brother Phocus (11.267–70; cf. 7.669–71) and prefaces Alcyone's first appearance with another episode of a supernatural predator, a wolf destroying Peleus's cattle (11.379–84). As Ceyx is preparing to join a punitive expedition, Alcyone rushes in begging him not to go but stay and, by saving his own life, save hers also. This is the highly emotional language of Roman elegy and prepares the readers for renewed anguish.

This is a false alarm: Ceyx reassures her (11.389–92) that he will not join the wolf hunt because he must supplicate Thetis, whom Peleus has offended. And Thetis responds, turning the wolf, like the Theban fox of Cephalus's tale, into marble. But unfortunately, the pious Ceyx is still troubled by another family sorrow, the metamorphosis of his angry brother Daedalion (11.290–345), and tells his wife that he must sail to Claros in Asia Minor to consult Apollo. Ovid stresses this moment by writing from Alcyone's viewpoint, sharing her terrors as she grows pale and weeps, almost unable to protest at the risk to her husband. She dreads the wanton violence of the winds, whom her father, Aeolus, can barely control, and begs Ceyx, if he must sail, to let her go with him: "Together what may come we both shall bear, / Together on the wide seas we shall fare" (11.441–2, tr. Melville). He promises to return, and she follows his ship as he sets out, collapsing when she can no longer see it.

Inevitably, the ship is destroyed by a powerful storm, which Ovid describes in virtuoso detail, and Ceyx is drowned, murmuring "Alcyone" until the wild waters overwhelm him. (In fact, Ovid deliberately uses the phrase "Alcyone is on his lips" [11.544] to recall Cephalus's protestation that he kept Procris ever on his lips [7.708].) All this time Alcyone prays constantly to Juno for her husband's safe return, but once he is drowned Juno finds the prayers intolerable and sends Iris to ask the god of sleep to send Alcyone a dream in the form of Ceyx to reveal his death to her. (We shall return to Sleep and the world of dreams in ch. 8.) The dream impersonator Morpheus appears to the sleeping Alcyone, swearing he is Ceyx and asking her to give him ritual lament so that he will not go to Hades unmourned.

There are many ancient poems mourning those drowned at sea; the worst aspect of such a death was the loss of the body, which deprived the corpse of burial and the mourners of completing their ritual. As the deceptive dream-ghost prepares to depart, Alcyone begs him, as she had done when Ceyx departed, to stay or let her come with him (676). Convinced she has seen her drowned husband, she rushes at dawn to the pier where she last saw Ceyx. There she sees a body being carried on the water, which is gradually revealed as Ceyx, and she cries out, evoking his last promise. "Is this how you return to me, my dear and pitiable beloved?" This is when the miracle occurs. As she leaps from the pier, hoping to die near him, Alcyone begins to fly, crying out piteously, and she reaches and embraces the chill body. Yet onlookers believe the dead Ceyx felt her kisses. The gods take pity (this is the third time in this love story that Ovid has invoked the concept of pity) and Ceyx too is transformed into a halcyon bird. The pair cherish their love together and reproduce, hatching their young on miraculously calm seas each winter while Alcyone's father, Aeolus, restrains the winds from rampaging in storm.

Ovid has found many ways of steeping this miniature epic in emotion: Ceyx himself is both devout and troubled by grief for his brother Daedalion; Alcyone, from beginning to end, is moved only by anxious love for her husband. The poet repeatedly puts expressions of devotion and then grief into her mouth so that his audience must share her emotions: neither the terrible storm and shipwreck in the central part of the narrative nor the mysterious house of Sleep and his specialized dreams allow the readers to forget husband and wife. As with the innocent Baucis and Philemon, transformation is salvation, guaranteeing continued union, but instead of inanimate trees, these lovers are sentient and reproductive birds, protected by the very elements that destroyed the human Ceyx. Cephalus's strange tale of jealousy and intrigue found no better resolution than his reassurance to his dying wife of his lasting love. We may feel that he did not deserve the release of sharing her death. Certainly, Ovid shows by his treatment of these stories of married love (and we might add the love of Cadmus and Harmonia, 4.583–603) that he could see no happier end than a shared transformation from human consciousness. There is no clearer proof that in its idealized form metamorphosis was seen as escape from both life and death.

Further Reading

Brooks Otis, *Ovid as an Epic Poet,* 2d ed. (Cambridge, 1970); Stephen Hinds, "Medea in Ovid: Scenes from the Life of an Intertextual Heroine," *Materiali e Dicussioni* 30 (1993): 9–47; Carole E. Newlands, "The Metamorphosis of Ovid's Medea," in *Medea: Essays on*

Medea in Myth, Literature, Philosophy, and Art, ed. J. J. Claus and S. I. Johnston (Princeton, 1997), 178–208; R. J. Tarrant, "The Silence of Cephalus: Text and Narrative Technique in Ovid, *Metamorphoses* 7.685ff.," *Transactions of the American Philological Association* 125 (1995): 99–111; N. Gregson Davis, *The Death of Procris: "Amor" and the Hunt in Ovid's "Metamorphoses"* (Rome, 1983).

·7·

Heroes—Old Style and New

The Earliest Greek Heroes

Ovid's *Metamorphoses* derives much of its vitality from the poet's sheer delight in adventure, and many of the most colorful tales are of the old pre-Homeric heroes, who were sent on missions or wandered the Greek world when it was still underpopulated, confronting monsters and ridding local communities of brigands and pests. We have already met the dragon that consumed Cadmus's men when he came to Boeotia to found the city of Thebes, and the heroes of Ovid's poem hunt down and exterminate other, more conventional pests, such as the fox that Cephalus hunted for the Boeotians, the wolf that preyed on Peleus's flocks in Thessaly, and most memorably the boar sent by Diana to ravage Calydon, which is hunted by all the brightest and best young warriors of Greece.

While the term "hero" properly meant the son of a god and a mortal, not all heroes had a divine parent. Of the classic adventurers Ovid gives varying degrees of attention to four heroes: Perseus, son of Jupiter and Danae; Theseus, son of Neptune and Aethra; Jason, son of mortal parents; and Hercules (Greek Herakles), son of Jupiter and Alcmene. But while Greek and Roman audiences may have loved suspenseful accounts of heroic combats like that of Cadmus and the dragon, Ovid took these stories up only if they offered a chance for novelty and a satisfying display of *virtus*, "masculinity," shown in ingenuity or daring. Jason is an exception to this pattern because Ovid's focus on the skills of the barbarian princess Medea diminishes Jason's role in the quest for the golden fleece: so when she has guided him through the ordeals and killed the dragon guardian to recover the fleece, he is awarded the title of "heroic son of Aeson" (7.156), but it is Medea who wins the glory.

Perseus, on the other hand, offered scope for novelty because of the technical challenge afforded by his primary adversary, the Gorgon Medusa, and his subsequent exploitation of her as a secret weapon. Here is a questing hero who is equipped with supernatural mobility and participates in an exploit involving both aspects of the gaze: the deadly gaze of Medusa and Perseus's own lovesick gaze upon Andromeda, tethered to a sea crag, whose statue-like beauty is almost an inversion of his old enemy. Of the three Gorgon sisters, Medusa was the only mortal, coiffed with venomous snakes and able to turn to stone whoever looked at her. But Perseus in turn had divine gifts of high-tech weaponry for his assault on her: from Athena, a polished shield in which he could see the reflection of Medusa's deadly gaze unharmed, and from Mercury, winged sandals for a vertical approach and a curved blade with which to strike Medusa at an angle.

Since this might make his victory seem too easy, Ovid introduces Perseus after he has slain the Gorgon, when he is overflying Libya, carrying her head under a protective hood (4.615: it is the blood dripping from her throat that gives birth to the many serpents of Libya). Instead of the famous combat, Ovid reports two magical African adventures. The first begins when Perseus reaches the home of Atlas, king of the west, and asks for hospitality, identifying himself as son of Jupiter. This would normally ensure a courteous reception, but unfortunately, Atlas had been given a prophecy that his golden apples would be stolen by a son of Jupiter (so they would— by Hercules) and so refused to admit Perseus, who retaliated by confronting him with the Gorgon's head and thus brought into being the Atlas mountain range (4.631–52).

Later, as he approaches Ethiopia on his way east, Perseus catches sight of Andromeda, bound and exposed on a cliff as food for a sea monster, and instantly falls in love (and almost out of the sky, 677). Perhaps for her sake, he does not use the Gorgon's powers, but dive-bombs the sea monster, stabbing it with his curved sword. Thrashing wildly around, it sprays Perseus's winged sandals, making them waterlogged, which reduces Perseus to fighting from ground level: landing on a crag, he clings to it with his left hand as he four times drives his curved sword through the monster's loins. Naturally, he is hailed as savior by Andromeda's parents, who offer him her hand in marriage.

Book 4 seems to be moving toward closure, with the happy couple all set to live happily ever after. Indeed, Perseus, "conqueror of the snake-locked Gorgon" and soon to be dignified as "the heroic son of Danae" (5.1), is entertaining the wedding guests with his previous adventures and the origin of Medusa's petrifying beauty when his enemy and rival Phineus bursts into the hall at the head of a hostile retinue. In the battle that follows, Perseus is unarmed, but Ovid gives him a fight sequence of vivid killings (the sort of display of prowess which connoisseurs of Homer call an *aristeia*). He would even have killed Phineus outright with the villain's own spear if he had not ducked behind the altar (5.36–7). Pallas Athene is there to protect her "brother" (they are both children of Jupiter), and Perseus dispatches a large number of lesser enemies with whatever weapon is to hand: a wedding torch (57–8), his curved blade (69–70), a massive mixing bowl with projecting relief figures (81–3), and a little later a spear that he has wrenched out of another man's wound (137–8).

As Phineus with a thousand men converges on the lone warrior (157), Perseus fights on in conventional combat until he feels his *virtus* fail; only then does he resort (177) to the head of Medusa. There are now two hundred survivors, and as each approaches and taunts Perseus, he is petrified in a striking pose until they are all frozen into statues (208). Now Phineus, with the pathos of Virgil's Turnus, renounces his claim to Andromeda, asking only for his life, to which Perseus scornfully offers as "a great concession for such a coward" that he will not be wounded by any steel but become a household ornament for his father-in-law. The new statue of Phineus kneeling in supplication (5.232–5) is the last vignette of Perseus's saga.

Although Theseus had triumphed over a number of nasty brigands on his way from Troezen to Athens, he was more of a local hero, and his feats may have offered less scope for the imagination. We only meet him, like Perseus, after his combats, when he has cleansed the Isthmus of crime (7.404–5). His first ordeal on arrival at his father's palace is to escape attempted poisoning by Medea, now his stepmother, with aconite, a new poison that requires a narrative flashback to one of Hercules' labors. He had been commanded by Juno and Eurystheus to fetch the guard dog Cerberus from Hades, and traditionally it was on this mission that he rescued Theseus from imprisonment there—a story quite incompatible with Ovid's version here. Instead, Ovid concentrates on the origin of the poison as foam from Cerberus's jaws, cheating his audience of their expectations. Ovid then returns to the Theseus story: at the last minute Aegeus recognizes Theseus's sword as a family heirloom. Father and son are united and the wicked stepmother put to flight. In the general rejoicing Ovid compresses Theseus's heroic record into a hymn (7.433–50) enumerating the lands he has freed from pests and brigands, which ends in a suspiciously modern imperial style with "if we wanted to list your titles, your achievements would outnumber your years. Gallant hero, we offer public vows on your behalf, and drain bumpers of wine."

One reason that we hear less of Theseus's heroic combats is that, to quote Keith (1999: 223) "Ovid prefers to explore the construction of masculinity within groups of men, the epic hero's competition for preeminence among his fellows." In book 8 Theseus leaves Athens to join the more than thirty heroes who combine in the hunt for the Calydonian boar, in which his only initiative is more romantic than heroic, as he advises his partner, Peirithous, "dear heart, dearer than my own self, half of my soul, stop! Brave men may keep their distance: Ancaeus suffered for his rash display of manliness" (8.405–7). But Theseus's advice is in keeping with the farcical tone of the whole boar hunt, which comes nearer to burlesque than epic.

First, Ovid unfolds the reason for the hunt: a swine (Latin *sus* is as down-to-earth as my translation) sent against Calydon as both agent and avenger of angry Diana. King Oeneus had sacrificed to every patron god but her, and the poet quotes her furious reaction: "we won't let this go unpunished . . . we may be called unhonored, but never unavenged!" (8.279–80). The boar's flashing tusks and destructive assaults on grain, grape, olive, and cattle are described in loving detail, until Meleager assembles his band of heroes flushed with love of glory. The divine Dioscuri are there and all the Argonauts; in fact, the hunting party is a virtual roll call of the young warriors from the generation before Troy. The poet lavishes rich language on describing the woods in which the hunters gather with nets and hounds, and the marsh in which they corner the boar: this was a scene many upper-class Romans had enjoyed and would recognize.

The first two spears, however, miss their quarry, and Diana knocks the tip off the third, which only enrages the beast. The wound-inflicting boar (Ovid mocks Ennian diction with *vulnificus sus,* 359) lays low two heroes, who are carried off wounded, while another perishes hamstrung. The great names of Homer's epic are humiliated, as Nestor escapes by pole-vaulting on his spear into a tree, and even the Dioscuri—those future constellations, advancing breast to breast, handsome on their snow-white steeds, and brandishing their spears—were unable to wound the bristly creature because it plunged into dark woods impassable to horse or spear (372–7). Telamon caps this by tripping over the root of a tree and has to be picked up by Peleus. The lovesick Meleager greets with rapture the slight nick beneath the boar's ear inflicted by the glamorous Atalanta (381–3), while Ancaeus, provoked by the girl's success, defies Diana, boasting that a real man with men's weapons will easily finish off the beast. As he raises his battle-axe to slay it, the beast gores him with its tusks where his manhood is most vulnerable and he collapses in a pool of blood. It is at this moment that Theseus decides discretion is the better part of valor. The farce is turning sour, as the frustration of so many failures drives the band of brothers to violence and causes the murderous quarrel between Meleager and his uncles that drives his mother to bring about his death. (We will postpone to ch. 8 comment on the battle between the Lapiths and the centaurs, which adds the novelty of centaur cavalry-fighting to its similar mixture of heroism and farce.)

Old and New Versions of Hercules

A thenian legend often represented Hercules and Theseus fighting as allies or gave Theseus a share in the traditional achievements of Hercules. But Ovid may have reversed the flow in one respect, for he has given the Athenians a formal hymn of praise to Theseus modeled on Virgil's hymn to Hercules in *Aeneid* 8: there Evander's Arcadians commemorate the anniversary of his victory over the demon Cacus (8.293–302). The life of Hercules included too many labors for Ovid to do them justice without unbalancing his narrative. But the Romans had adopted the cult of Hercules before any other Greek cult, and the "unconquered" son of Jupiter and Theban Alcmene was virtually a Roman himself. How would Ovid determine Hercules' share of his sweep through prehistory?

We have seen that Ovid's Perseus and Theseus sagas both introduced allusions to labors of Hercules. His local chores cleansing the Peloponnese of hydras and lions and swamp birds and stags—not to mention mucking out Augeas's stables—had long since been augmented by stories pitting him against Amazons beyond the Black Sea, tyrants in Egypt and Thrace, and giants in Libya and Spain. His Pillars (Gibraltar and Ceuta [Tangier]) guarded the entrance to the Mediterranean. But Ovid's narrative was firmly set in mainland Greece, and he did not want to follow Hercules to Italy; indeed, he had no doubt already assigned the duel with Cacus to its place in his Roman calendar, the *Fasti*. So he confines himself to one hand-to-hand combat—against the river Achelous—a story told by Achelous himself to Theseus, among others, around the river god's dinner table. Once again the viva voce report of a participant gives narrative immediacy (8.880–5; 9.4–86).

Ovid's focus is as much on Achelous's own unusual fighting methods as on Hercules, for the river god can change his shape into that of a serpent or bull. They fight as rival suitors for Deianeira, with all the trappings of a conventional wrestling bout. Achelous asks his audience to believe that, although he lost this battle, Hercules tried three times to break his hold before he succeeded; at that point, recognizing, like Perseus, that he was losing the fight (9.62, cf. 5.177), Achelous resorted to shape-shifting, slithering out from Hercules' grasp in serpent form—but, as Hercules points out, he had strangled serpents in his cradle, and one measly serpent is only a fraction of the hundred-headed hydra! Achelous's final bull shape also fails, when Hercules forces him to the ground and breaks off his horn.

The purpose of the river god's story is to explain the origin of the horn of plenty, whose exemplar was his own broken horn, which the nymphs filled with fruit. But its appeal lies in Ovid's ability to give a professional account of a wrestling match, which I cannot imitate. From this victory the poet leads naturally into the treacherous attempt of the centaur Nessus to rape Hercules' bride, Deianeira, while he is ferrying her across the swollen river Evenus. Ovid's readers knew the outcome: when Hercules pierced the centaur with an arrow smeared with the poisonous blood of the Hydra, Nessus in turn revenged himself by giving Deianeira his garment soaked in this poison and his own venomous blood and claiming it as a love charm (9.101–33). Thus, to mention Nessus was to anticipate the occasion of Hercules' death, when his wife Deianeira believed he had taken the captive princess Iole as his mistress and sent him the poisoned robe to win back his love. Ovid moves quickly from the rumor of Hercules' infidelity to Deianeira's anguish and the sending of the robe.

The death of Hercules has an importance beyond its own melodrama. Here, in the ninth book of his world history, Ovid will present the first real deification of a mortal. His narrative combines the appeal of a horror story with the function of preparing the way for Rome's own deified heroes, starting from Aeneas. Hercules was sacrificing when he put on the robe (9.151), and as he poured the libation of wine, the poison seethed and broke into flames, engulfing his limbs. He kicked over the altar in his agony and bellowed as he tried to pull away the robe, which instead tore away his flesh. His blood hissed like red-hot steel tempered in icy water, and sweat streamed from his body. At this climax Ovid breaks off to give Hercules a denunciation of his enemy Juno, as he begs for death. But the protest turns into an enumeration of his many heroic labors (182–200), starting with his slaughter of Busiris, who polluted altars with the blood of innocent foreigners. The more familiar labors are turned into allusive tests of the readers' learning, as, for example, the three-bodied Geryon and three-headed Cerberus are packaged together (185: *forma triplex*), and the stables of Augeas are implied only by "Elis has the work of my hands." Ovid keeps almost to the end Diomedes of Thrace, as vicious as Busiris, who fattened his mares on human flesh: "I gazed on the stables full of torn human bodies and demolished them, destroying both horses and master."

There is only one triumph we probably should not credit to Ovid. In *Aeneid*, Virgil had made Evander's people add Hercules' victory over Cacus as a postscript to his other noble deeds. Someone has inserted into Ovid's text "With these hands the dreadful monster Cacus [lies strangled] on the Tiber shore," but the line is probably not by Ovid himself, who confines himself here to Hercules' record in the Greek world.

Ironically, Hercules' last words argue from the injustice of his suffering and Eurystheus's survival to rejecting belief in the existence of the gods (9.204–5). But he is not far from becoming one, as he stalks Mount Oeta stretching out his arms to his father's heavenly home. Seeing Lichas, who brought him the robe, he hurls the youth into the sea, where he becomes a rock. Then, after constructing a pyre, Hercules entrusts his bow and arrows to the loyal Philoctetes (line 232 looks forward to the part played by the bow and Philoctetes himself in the second conquest of Troy) and spreads his lion skin over the pyre, reclining on it with his club as pillow as if he were a dinner guest lying garlanded among the wine cups (as Hercules only too often had been).

The hero's new Stoic calm is a cue for panic in heaven, as the gods fear for the "liberator" of the earth (9.241). It is in response to their fear that Jupiter now takes control, reading their concern for his son as loyalty to him, their ruler and father (familiar political language at Rome). Graciously acknowledging their support as a tribute to Hercules but also a service to himself, Jupiter reassures them: "Hercules, who has won all battles, will win again, and only his mortal mother's part will feel Vulcan's power. What he has inherited from me is immortal, immune to death and indestructible by any fire. Now that the immortal part has completed its task on earth, I shall welcome him to the heavenly regions, which I know will bring joy to all the gods—or if anyone is grieved by Hercules as a god, he will know that this reward is deserved and reluctantly give his approval" (9.250–8).

The gods know their part and agree (9.259, cf. 1.244–5), even Juno, offended by the last remark, which is formulated in the masculine gender but clearly aimed at her. Now comes Hercules' transfiguration (the highest kind of metamorphosis) as Vulcan burns away his mortal dross and he emerges gleaming like a serpent:

> Shining resplendent in his sleek new scales,
> So Hercules, his mortal frame removed,
> Through all his finer parts gained force and vigour,
> In stature magnified, transformed into
> A presence clothed in majesty and awe. (9.266–70,
>   tr. Melville)

Here then is Rome's first human god, and we should note two phrases that Ovid has worked into his glorification of the hero. First, his "finer parts" survive death, just as Ovid will claim the survival of his poetry as his own finer part in his triumphant epilogue. Second, when Ovid describes Hercules as "clothed in majesty and awe," the words he uses are *augusta gravitate verendus,* "revered for august greatness" (270), which would be understood by Ovid's readers as giving him the qualities of Augustus himself. Romans did not distinguish proper names from adjectives by capitalization, and Ovid has chosen the word to evoke his emperor. He is inviting his readers to see in the transfigured Hercules a foreshadowing of Rome's present imperial ruler, known since 27 B.C.E. as Augustus, and in Greek as Sebastos, Latin *verendus*.

Roman affection for Hercules, and perhaps a desire for continuity, lead Ovid to prolong the hero's presence in the text even after his death. His sack of Troy when King Laomedon denied him the reward for driving away Neptune's sea monster provided continuity, for Hercules had spared Laomedon's little son Priam in his conquest, so that Priam and his city were both captured twice. But Hercules had also waged war on Messenia, and Ovid integrates both feats into a later context through a conversational exchange between the aged Nestor of Pylos and Hercules' son Tlepolemos, after a feast early in the Trojan War. Nestor has recalled at great length the battle between the Lapiths and the drunken centaurs at the wedding of Peirithoos. Tlepolemus breaks in to remind Nestor that his father defeated the centaurs, and Nestor answers sadly that it pains him to recall Hercules, who destroyed his own city of Pylos and his home, killing his eleven brothers (12.537–55: both these feats of Hercules are mentioned by the same speaker in the *Iliad*). In fact, Ovid contrives a certain symmetry, because the last story he associates with Hercules is his defeat and killing of another shapeshifter, as he defeated but spared Achelous. When he attacked Nestor's brother Periclymenos, Periclymenos transformed himself into an eagle and was miraculously shot down by the arrows of Hercules. The stories emphasize the aged Nestor's generous forgiveness of his suffering in a past generation.

The other hero who carries Ovid's narrative up to the siege of Troy is of course Achilles, the first great hero of epic poetry. Ovid did not set himself up to compete with Homer in artistry, any more than he would compete with Virgil in presenting his hero Aeneas. Instead, Ovid focuses on one of Achilles' early triumphs: his combat with the supposedly invincible warrior Cycnus, son of Neptune. Cycnus is actually no more invincible than Caeneus (whom we met in ch. 5) but is impervious to weapons; Achilles strips him of his helmet and strangles him with his bare hands. But, as with Nessus and Hercules, the early combat introduces the first cause of Achilles' death. In Ovid's version—and this seems to be his own invention— it is Cycnus's father, Neptune, who now engineers Achilles' death by conspiring with Apollo to redirect the cowardly archer Paris against the hero. Urged on by Apollo, Paris shoots and Apollo makes sure that his aim in unerring (12.585–611).

Within a single book Ovid has carried history forward through ten years and beyond the *Iliad* to the aftermath of Achilles' death. Book 13 opens with the bitter eloquence of two Homeric heroes, Ajax and Odysseus, competing for the prize of his weapons (13.1– 395), and marks the extinction of Priam's dynasty. But now it is as though Ovid's epic has changed sides, for the next hero, the survivor from Troy, is a new kind of hero and Rome's own future founder.

Heroes of Rome: The Civic Leader and Apotheosis

The walls of Troy are overthrown, but the gods sustain its future hope, sending out the hero born of Venus who will lead the Trojan people safely to Latium and father the royal line of Rome's founder, Romulus. Aeneas departs with his son Ascanius, carrying the local gods of the city and his father, and moves through the first stages of his journey westward to Delos (13.623–31). Although Ovid follows their journey through the next book, it is always at a distance, marking only the landfalls and leaving the main narrative to explore less heroic tales of subsidiary characters, so that even Aeneas's final victory over his enemy Turnus in single combat is described in indirect and passive form: Venus sees her son's arms victorious, and Turnus dies, as does his city (14.572–80).

Although we have seen little of Virgil's hero in this narrative, Ovid now reaches Aeneas's big moment, one only forecast by Virgil's epic. When Aeneas's valor (not his piety, as Virgil would have said) had conciliated even Juno, and his growing son Iulus was already gaining in wealth and power, his father, the hero born of

Venus (14.584: Ovid echoes his introductory phrase from 13.625), was now ripe for heaven. Now it was time and Venus canvassed the gods and embraced her father Jupiter, begging for his son to be rewarded with godhead—even a minor form of godhead. (As always when he is dealing with Venus, Ovid manages to suggest a shallow and foolish woman.) As with Jupiter's "request" for Hercules, so now the gods give approval (592), and even Juno is reconciled. Continuing the parade of democracy, Jupiter now confirms that her request is granted, and Venus flies in her dove-drawn chariot to the river Numicius, where she orders the river to cleanse Aeneas of all his mortal elements and carry him down to the sea. As with Hercules, his best part survives. His mother anoints him with ambrosia and makes him a god, hailed as "Indiges" by the people of Quirinus and assigned his own temple and altars.

This new-style hero, then, is not shown in heroic action; his deeds are treated as known, and Ovid concentrates on his transformation into a god. He will do the same for Rome's first king, Romulus. Again, the hero's main achievements are detached from him and indirectly expressed: "Old Numitor recovers his kingdom by the gift of his grandson, and the city walls are founded on the feast day of the Parilia" (14.773−5). Then, after a helpful obstruction by the nymphs (who turn their spring to sulfurous fire), which enables Romulus to defeat the invading Sabines and make a treaty of reconciliation, Ovid comes almost immediately to the scene of Romulus's death (forty years on) as he administers the law. Relying on his established pattern, the poet once again invokes a divine parent, but this time he can cite poetic precedent. Mars, Romulus's divine father, approaches Jupiter just as he had done in Ennius's great epic, *Annals of Rome,* and reminds him that he had promised him his son's deification in front of the divine council. Mars has even recorded Jupiter's words and repeats the key line from Ennius: "there shall be one / whom you shall raise to the blue vault of heaven" (14.812−5). Like Aeneas, the hero has completed his task and Rome is secure; the time has come, and Jupiter consents, covering the earth with cloud. Mars gathers Romulus into his chariot; his mortal body dissolves in the thin air and is replaced by a noble appearance, more worthy of the couches of the gods. Ovid compares his new appearance to the kilted statue of Quirinus (827–8), a mysterious god of Sabine origin whom the Romans had come to identify with their deified first king. Romulus's wife, the Sabine Hersilia, becomes the goddess Hora and is joined as consort to Quirinus (851).

How does Ovid maintain this decorous distance from his heroes as history comes close to his own time? He evades chronology by sending Romulus's successor, Numa, to learn about the universe from the Greek philosopher Pythagoras (who flourished a century after Numa's death) and by introducing the prehistoric Hippolytus ("the hero born of Theseus," 15.492) in a very posthumous conversation with Numa's divine consort, Egeria. Between this episode and Ovid's own time come two strange stories, of a Roman leader, Cipus, who does not become a god, and of a divine immigrant to Rome, Aesculapius, who travels from Greece in the fabulous form of a serpent. Both stories are found in Valerius Maximus, writing after Ovid. The coming of Aesculapius goes back to Livy, and so may the politically pointed story of Cipus, which is told by Valerius with details independent of Ovid.

The tale of Cipus is also a fantasy imposed on history (15.565–621). The popular Roman general was returning from victory over Rome's enemies when he discovered horns on his forehead and consulted a diviner. The diviner hails him as king and congratulates him because Rome and Latium will become subject to him once he has returned within the city walls. Horrified, the good republican decides he would prefer exile to the evil of being a king, and he summons the senate and people outside the walls to warn them that someone among them will become king and make them his subjects unless they expel him: they will know this man by his horns. When Cipus removes the laurel wreath that conceals his horns, the Romans groan and set a festal garland on his head. And since he felt bound to stay outside the walls, they gave him as much land as plow-oxen could encircle within a day and carved horns on the posts of the city gate in his honor.

The tale is a typical explanation of a local monument, but why does Ovid include it here? He has not formally commemorated the expulsion of the kings and the founding of the republic (treated at length in book 2 of his *Fasti*), so that we pass suddenly from the good kings Romulus and Numa to a time when the name of king is dreaded, and true heroism consists, like that of Regulus, in sacrificing oneself to Roman liberty and honor. Cipus had effectively refused the title of king. And so had Julius Caesar, who regularly wore the triumphant general's laurel wreath and is separated from Cipus in Ovid's narrative only by the fantastic voyage and coming of the serpent god. Ovid did not need to remind his fellow Romans that Julius Caesar had publicly refused the diadem, symbol of kingship, shortly before his death. (He had in fact chosen instead a dictatorship for life, scarcely less alarming to republican thinking.)

Instead of contrasting Caesar with Cipus, Ovid contrasts him with Aesculapius as a homegrown god, deified in his own city. Yet it was not Caesar's victories over Britain and Egypt and Numidia and Pontus that earned him godhead. Nor was it a divine parent—the pattern we have come to expect. No! It was his (adopted) son who turned him into a new star, the comet that was seen at Rome after Caesar's death. But then his son was Caesar's greatest achievement (15.745–59). We have come back to the here-and-now and to the need for courtly panegyric.

Inverting the previous pattern of deification, Ovid now argues that Caesar had to be made a god so that his son, Augustus, would have a divine father. As he tells the tale, Venus, the ancestress of the Julii, saw that a conspiracy was bringing near Caesar's death, and she appealed to all the gods, complaining of the treachery being organized against her and urging them to save Vesta's high priest. This time there is no divine council, but we are assured that the gods all grieved, sending dreadful portents (15.780–98; cf. 1.200–203). But they could not break the decrees of the fatal sisters. In despair Venus is preparing to rescue Caesar (as she had Aeneas) in a cloud, when Jupiter intercepts her, reassuring her with a massive speech designed to recall his prophetic affirmations to Venus in the first book of the *Aeneid* (15.807–42). This serves the dual purpose of embedding the exaltation of Augustus within the Julian context and of sparing the poet anything so blatant as a direct encomium. Jupiter tells Venus that the fate of her descendants is already assured, inscribed by the Fates in their monumental archive. Now that Julius has fulfilled his destiny, she and his own son will ensure that he becomes a god. After Caesar's death, his son will take on unaided the burden of Caesar's responsibilities and avenge his father's murder. There follows Jupiter's guarantee of what is still to come: the continued beneficent achievements of Augustus himself and his dynasty, until late in time he too will finally join the stars.

Prophecy returns to narrative. Given her authorization, Venus descends unseen and snatches Caesar's soul from his wounded body, but the heavenly spirit ignites, to fly high above the moon, trailing a comet tail, and to contemplate his son's glorious deeds on earth. Finally, the poet reiterates in his own person (whatever his private convictions may have been) that the son has proved greater than the father and prays to all the appropriate civic gods for blessings on Augustus and Rome (15.852–70).

We have come a long way from the swashbuckling Greek heroes, and many readers will regret the conversion to the new national ideal, focused on formal leadership and public acclaim. Virgil had escaped this only by imposing closure on his great epic before the official happy ending, but it is difficult to see that Ovid thirty years later had any other option. The question was not what he should say in praise of Augustus but how he could present it to his readers as a logical but memorable culmination of his journey through history.

Further Reading

A. Keith, "Versions of Epic Masculinity in Ovid's *Metamorphoses*," in *Ovidian Transformations: Essays on Ovid's "Metamorphoses" and Its Reception*, ed. Philip R. Hardie, Alessandro Barchiesi, and Stephen Hinds (Cambridge, 1999), 214–39 (on Perseus, 221–3; on the boar hunt, 223–9; on the Lapiths and Centaurs, 234–7). See also N. Horsfall, "Epic and Burlesque in Ovid *Met.* viii 260ff.," *Classical Journal* 74 (1979): 319–32. On Hercules, see Stephen M. Wheeler, *A Discourse of Wonders: Audience and Performance in Ovid's "Metamorphoses"*

(Philadelphia, 1999), 135–9; P. R. Hardie, *The Epic Successors of Virgil: A Study in the Dynamics of a Tradition* (Cambridge, 1993), 65–7. On Aeneas and apotheosis, see K. S. Myers, *Ovid's Causes: Cosmogony and Aetiology in the "Metamorphoses"* (Ann Arbor, 1994); Garth Tissol, *The Face of Nature: Wit, Narrative, and Cosmic Origins in Ovid's "Metamorphoses"* (Princeton, 1997).

· 8 ·

Fantasy, the Fabulous,
and the Miraculous
Metamorphoses of Nature

Monsters and Marvels

Ancient myth and modern science fiction have in common their special ingredients of the fabulous, the miraculous, and the monstrous. These three adjectives all have Latin roots and go back to classical ideas about the license of different genres to indulge in fantasy. Roman rhetoric, for example, distinguished true historical narratives and plausible comic narratives from fabulous stories that were neither true nor plausible, citing as an example of the latter Medea's "huge winged dragons yoked to a car" from Ennius's tragedy. But even tragedy could only exploit the miraculous or marvelous as part of the plot, not part of the staged action. When Horace forbids the tragic playwright to show the offensive or the grotesque, his two examples are metamorphoses later used by Ovid: of Procne turning into a bird and of Cadmus into a snake. And metamorphosis itself is clearly monstrous, in both Roman senses: we think of a monster as some hybrid creature not normally found in nature, but for Romans a *monstrum* was primarily a supernatural event, a portent sent by the gods to show (*monstrare*) or warn (*monere*) men against dangerous behavior. So both the half-formed natural creatures found growing in the Nile mud (1.434–37) and the transformation of Phaethon's sisters into poplars (2.367) are called *monstra*. But so are the dragons and sea monsters defeated by Cadmus and Perseus and the tame dragon of the golden fleece.

In Plato's *Phaedrus,* when Socrates finds himself on the very spot where the winged Boreas supposedly carried off Princess Orithyia (described in *Met.* 6.702–10), he mentions the possibility of "saving" the myth by rationalization (the princess was carried away by a hurricane) but points out that a rationalizer would also have to explain away "centaurs and the chimaera, not to mention a whole host of such creatures, Gorgons and Pegasuses and countless other remarkable monsters of legend" (*Phaedr.* 229de).

In other words, the *Metamorphoses* is a "discourse of wonders," to quote the title of a fine recent study, and derives much of its appeal to our imagination from impossible events and beings that are neither human nor god nor beast. When Glaucus the fisherman transforms himself into a marine creature by eating magic seaweed, the nymph Scylla wonders whether this merman with blue beard and fishy tail is a god or a monster (13.912). Taking a cue from the ancient critics, let us consider the use Ovid makes, first, of some fabulous activities—flying and rejuvenation by witchcraft—and then of some fabulous creatures, the breed of centaurs.

First comes flying. Socrates jibbed at the myth of Boreas's rape of an Athenian princess but does not mention its extension by the birth of the winged twins, to which Ovid adds a pretense of plausibility by claiming that the twins developed wings, like secondary sexual characteristics, only when they reached puberty (6.716–8). We have, of course, accepted winged Olympians since Mercury first appeared, putting on his winged sandals to swoop to earth and taking them off when he disguises himself as a shepherd (1.671–5). In book 2 Ovid expands a vivid account of him looking down on earth and changing course when he sees the beautiful princesses, hovering in the air like a hawk over his prey (2.714–21). Similarly, after Mercury equips Perseus with winged sandals, the poet notes how Perseus is so stunned by the beauty of the half-naked and chained Andromeda that he "almost forgot to fly" (4.676–7), but then he soars and dives expertly in order to overcome the sea monster (4.712–20). To judge from Homer, all gods can control their flight, but some seem to enjoy special equipment. Thus, Phaethon can attempt to follow the Sun's regular course through the air in the sun chariot, and it is the Sun who lends a serpent-driven chariot to his grandchild Medea in Ovid's narrative, as he does in Greek tragedy.

In Medea's case, Ovid does not invoke her use of the chariot until she has already amazed both the Thessalian spectators and his Roman readers by some extended magical feats. We do not know if earlier writers lingered over her rejuvenation of Jason's aged father (he is long dead in Apollonius), but Ovid makes it the central and longest episode (163–293) in his Medea narrative. With her cousin Circe, Medea is Ovid's best example of someone who practices witchcraft. Begged by Jason to save his ailing father, she waits for the full moon, then makes herself ritually pure before praying to Hecate, listing the miracles of domination over nature that the black powers have enabled her to accomplish. When she begs Hecate for magic juices, the stars twinkle to confirm divine assent, and her sky chariot is suddenly at her side (7.180–217). Pausing to pat the necks of her serpent team, she sets the reins in motion and spends nine days flying across Thessaly to gather herbs. So powerful are the herbs that their proximity rejuvenates her serpents. But she backs up her pharmacopoeia with altars to Hecate and Youth, a sacred bouquet garni, and trenches to catch the blood of the sheep she sacrifices, topped up with libations of wine and milk and an appeal to the infernal rulers not to take the old man's soul (238–50). Medicine follows religion as Medea puts the old man to sleep on the bed of herbs and purifies him with fire, water, and sulfur. The herbs boiling in her cauldron are reinforced with powerful animal parts taken from screech owls and werewolves, and tested when Medea stirs the brew with a dried-up olive branch, which bursts into leaf. Now she is ready to cut Aeson's throat and replace his blood with the potion. The old man loses forty years of decrepitude, recovering the physique of a man in his prime. Even the god Bacchus is amazed at the miracle of so great a portent (7.294), but

Medea merely exploits the fame of her supernatural achievement to commit the entirely natural murder of Jason's old enemy Pelias. The chariot that she used for leisured herb gathering she now needs to escape from the scenes of her crimes, first to Corinth, then from Corinth to Athens (392, 398). Her last escape from Athens and from retaliation for her attempt to poison Theseus comes when (like her cousin Circe) she employs spells to generate a protective mist; the chariot, though unmentioned, is probably on hand for her getaway.

Having exploited the mystery of supernatural flight, Ovid adopts a very different tone for his last major flight narrative, the story of Daedalus and Icarus. He had already told their story in the second book of his *Art of Love*. Daedalus is the model of human ingenuity, an engineer who can construct a model cow to enable Pasiphae to mate with the bull she lusts after, and an inextricable labyrinth to contain her monstrous hybrid offspring, the bull-man Minotaur (8.159–68; also see ch. 4). To escape his imprisonment, Daedalus constructs feathered wings for himself and his little son, chooses his altitude, and reaches his destination. It is Icarus who soars too high and drops helpless into the sea when the sun's heat melts the wax that binds his wings (8.188–235). The onlookers may believe they have seen gods flying overhead, but in this context of human pathos the poet avoids any note of fantasy and keeps close to the plausible.

Now consider in turn how Ovid exploits the mythical tradition of monsters and hybrid creatures. We saw in chapter 7 how the whole Perseus saga is full of supernatural creatures—first Medusa, with her power to petrify, and her offspring, the winged horse Pegasus and the monster Chrysaor, then the sea monster—followed by protracted demonstrations of Medusa's posthumous powers as Perseus's fatal weapon. So let us take a cue from Socrates and look at Ovid's centaurs. In Greek mythology the centaurs were of doubly unnatural origin, since their human ancestor, Ixion, begot Centaurus on a cloud, and Centaurus mated with a series of mares. But one centaur, Chiron, child of the nymph Phillyra and Saturn in the form of a stallion, was of a higher nature: he was immortal, wise, and benevolent and acted as teacher of music and medicine to Achilles and Jason. We meet him briefly in *Met.* 2 when Apollo gives Chiron his motherless child Aesculapius to rear, and Chiron's prophetic daughter Ocyroe begins to prophesy Aesculapius's illicit resurrection. Here, Ovid uses Chiron's nature only to play on the divine metamorphosis of his human daughter into a mare and on his frustrated desire for mortality and death.

Ovid treats the notorious drunken brawl of the centaurs with the Lapiths at the wedding of Peirithous and Hippodame in a more farcical mode. In Nestor's account, one centaur, Eurytion, was inflamed with wine and laid lecherous hands on the bride, leading to a general uproar. The wedding is set in a mountain cave, and for more than a hundred lines Ovid draws his humor from the improvised weapons (goblets, lampstands, altars, torches, even whole oak trees) hurled by the combatants, without differentiating the human from the half-animal brawlers. He delays exploiting the centaurs' physique for comic effect, limiting himself to four moments in the continuing battle, before and after the sentimental tale of the centaurs Cyllarus and Hylonome. At line 345 a Lapith leaps onto the back of the centaur Bianor, unaccustomed to any rider except himself (i.e., his own human torso); the Lapith rides by kneeing the centaur and grasping his hair as he smashes him across the face. In the melée another centaur rears up and tramples his enemy with his hooves.

Then, changing tone, the poet introduces a love story with an apostrophe to the doomed hero: "alas, Cyllarus, your beauty did not rescue you in battle—that is, if we admit beauty in such an animal nature." As if in a wedding song Ovid describes his manly golden beard and locks, his fine shoulders comparable to noble statues, and every human aspect of his body, "nor was the appearance of the horse flawed, or unworthy of the man. Complete him with a horse's neck and head and he would have been a fit mount for Castor, with firm back and lofty muscled breast, glossy black body, and white legs and tail. But though many females of his tribe desired him, only Hylonome won his love" (12.398–405). With equal humor Ovid describes the fine grooming (*cultus*) of his beloved, her well-combed hair, her use of floral perfume and twice-daily baths, and her selection of the most becoming animal skins for her clothing. In an idyll of mutual love the couple rove the mountains together, and together enter battle. But they are no sooner described than they perish, as Cyllarus is wounded in the breast by an arrow, and Hylonome, lamenting, catches his dying breath. After this *Liebestod,* like Thisbe, she snatches the weapon that killed him and falls upon it, embracing her husband at the last. The charm of the tale lies in its closeness to human romance.

But Nestor's reminiscences return instantly from pathos to mayhem, with two more plays on the horse-men, as Phaeocomes advances, wearing six lion-skins to cover both man and horse, and the four-footed Echeclus is speared by the Lapith Ampyx. Even so, Ovid seems to have thought the transgendered Caeneus, with whom Nestor begins and ends his reminiscences, more remarkable than the cloud-begotten hybrids of man and horse. In both the flight sequences and the tales of imaginary creatures, the poet decides for himself when he wants to take a fantastic element for granted, and when he will create humor or pathos by drawing out its implications.

Another Aspect of the Nonhuman:
Allegorical Personages

Before Ovid, epic might offer a brief picture of abstractions like "Strife," which Homer depicts reaching from earth to heaven as she strides in battle attending on Ares in *Iliad* 4, or the "Prayers" and "Sinful Madness" of *Iliad* 9.502–6. To persuade Achilles to accept Agamemnon's petition, Phoenix offers a moral allegory, describing Prayers as "daughters of mighty Zeus, wrinkled, lame, and squint-eyed, who take pains to follow Madness. But Madness is strong and swift, so that she runs ahead of them all and causes harm to men worldwide. Then they put things right in her wake." In the allegory a man is rewarded or punished according to the respect that he shows to these daughters of the god of justice.

Punishment and vengeance were likely to be personified as ugly and vicious spirits equipped with instruments of torture, as are Bios and Kratos (Violence and Strength) in *Prometheus Bound*. This is how Virgil describes the monstrous fury Allecto, summoned by Juno (7.324–40), but Ovid goes beyond him in sending Juno down to Hades for the fury Tisiphone and describing the Fury's dress and escort. Similarly, he constructs complex descriptions of abstract concepts, providing them with an appropriate retinue and dwelling place. (Such set-pieces are called *ekphrasis*.) The first two instances, Jealousy and Hunger, are embodiments of psychological misery that somewhat resemble each other. Thus, the house of Jealousy is filthy with black decay, set in a sunless valley, unrefreshed by any breeze, and chilly for lack of fire; in other words, Jealousy is shown as lacking in all natural comfort (2.760–4). Minerva wants to punish the guilty Aglauros for betraying her secret, but she cannot enter the house of Jealousy, and so she strikes the door open and sees its inmate feeding on vipers' flesh. True to her character Jealousy groans and sighs at the sight of the goddess's health and beauty. Ovid has postponed her portrait until now: she is pallid and skinny, with shifty eyes and discolored teeth; her breast is green with gall and her tongue steeped in venom. Sleepless from discontent at others' success, she is simultaneously her own torment, gnawing with criticism as she is gnawed with envy (775–82). At Minerva's command Jealousy clutches her thorny stick and follows, muttering. She tramples the fields and blights the crops wherever she treads until she reaches the bedchamber of Aglauros; then, like Virgil's demon Allecto, she attacks the sleeping girl, filling her breast with brambles and poison and pitch, and besets her mind with images of her sister's good fortune in being courted by Mercury until she smolders with a slow and flameless fire, like thorny weeds. So we see the vicious passion, first in isolation, then embodied in its human victim.

The poet uses a similar technique to introduce Hunger, summoned by Ceres through one of her nymphs to punish the blasphemous Erysichthon (8.780–95). Like Minerva, Ceres cannot risk the contamination of approaching the negative spirit of Hunger, so she describes to the nymph where to find her, in an icy barren region of Scythia, along with other evil beings, "Chill" and "Pallor" and "Shivering." Her instructions are that Hunger should enter the evil man and torment him. The nymph (who incidentally borrows Ceres' flying-serpent chariot) finds Hunger grubbing up roots with her bare nails and teeth, hollow-eyed and so thin that her bones and joints all protrude and she has a hole where there should be a stomach. So infectious is her aura that the messenger nymph begins to feel hungry and turns her snakes right around in retreat to Thessaly. Hunger obediently seizes hold of the sleeping Erysichthon and fills him with manic and ruinous greed (8.816–42).

In contrast, Ovid offers a far more appealing introduction to Sleep in the tale of Ceyx and Alcyone: embarrassed by Alcyone's prayers for her dead husband, Juno sends Iris to ask Sleep for a dream in which a shape-shifter disguised as the drowned Ceyx will explain his death to his wife. It is always a god or his representative who contacts the abstraction, but this time the abstraction proliferates itself. First comes the description of Sleep's deep cave near the legendary Cimmerians, where the sun never penetrates but mists exude from the ground in a dim twilight. There is no sound or movement except the flowing of Lethe, and there is a carpet of soporific plants which Night gathers to sprinkle over the earth. Inside the cave, Sleep rests under dusky coverlets on a deep-feathered ebony couch, surrounded by innumerable dreams (11.592–615). Pushing the dreams aside like bats or cobwebs, Iris casts an unaccustomed light, and the god with difficulty rouses himself, shaking himself (i.e., sleep) from his eyes. His visitor addresses Sleep with almost hymnic respect, delivers her message, and departs. Now Ovid lets his imagination rip, as he describes the dream impersonator Morpheus ("The shaper") commissioned by Sleep who can walk the walk and talk the talk of each man; not content, Ovid mentions other dream artists: one who can imitate bird or beast or snake, whom the gods call Icelos (Greek *eikelos*, the Likener) but mortals call Phobetor (Nightmare), and another, Phantasos, who specializes in imitating the inanimate; but the latter, we are told, only appears to high-class dreamers, while others visit the common people. Once Sleep has summoned Morpheus, he sinks back and buries his head in his bedclothes. We have already seen in chapter 6 how consummately Morpheus carries out his assignment with Alcyone.

Is it coincidence that Ovid does not openly compete with Virgil until he reaches the last of his extended personifications? Virgil had prefaced the collapse of Aeneas's relationship with Dido in *Aeneid* with a vivid portrait of Rumor, "swiftest of all evils, who thrives in action and gains strength as she goes, starting quite small, then soaring into the sky, and burying her head in the clouds as she treads on the ground." Virgil makes her the last child of an enraged Earth; she is "a huge loathsome monster with as many eyes and tongues and mouths and ears as she has feathers: this monster flies by night betwixt heaven and earth, never shutting her eyes in sleep; by day she crouches on a rooftop or high towers and terrifies mighty cities, as obsessed with distorted lies as she is a messenger of truth" (4.174–88). Rumor seems to be related to the screech owls, which Romans identified with witches, but she is also a two-way transmitter, listening for gossip as well as spreading it by mouth.

Ovid reserves his elaboration of this famous portrait for the opening of the Trojan War after the Greek fleet gathers at Aulis. Unlike his other personifications, Rumor (*fama*) is not activated by any divine superior. Instead, she is at the center of the earth listening in on and scrutinizing whatever happens. Her home is a citadel with a thousand open entrances; the whole building is made of echoing bronze, which repeats and echoes whatever it hears; inside there is no silence or repose but a constant murmuring like a distant sea or storm. Like a Roman senator's mansion, Rumor's halls are filled with a crowd that comes and goes, mixing with the truth thousands of fictitious tales that spread confusion. And, like the tales of Virgil's Fama, Rumor's lies are incessantly repeated, increasing the scale of falsehood, by her retinue of Credulity, rash Confusion, hollow Joy, panicked Terrors, fresh Disloyalty, and suspect Whispers. At the center of them all, she sees whatever happens in heaven and earth and sea and carries her investigations over the whole world (12.39–63).

But—anticlimactically—all Rumor achieves is to alert the Trojans to the actual approach of the Greek expedition. No rumor was needed, for the intent of the Greeks was well heralded across the Aegean. Where Virgil's Rumor brought catastrophe upon Dido and turned Aeneas back to his destiny, it would be hard to accept that Fama had prevented a Greek surprise victory. Soon after, when Cycnus, son of Neptune, tells Achilles that he knows him from Fama (12.86) and is himself immune to weapons, this too does not affect the outcome, either by giving Cycnus helpful knowledge (for instance, of Achilles' heel) or by saving him from death by suffocation. Where Jealousy, Hunger, and Sleep offered vivid food for the imagination and prepared the way for retribution or release from grief, the world information service of Rumor serves no narrative purpose.

The Miracles of Natural Change

Critics have expressed contrary views of the extraordinary lecture (or sermon) attributed to Pythagoras, yet its length and its position in the first half of the final book guarantee that Ovid saw it as an important part of the meaning of his poem. Of course, he knew, as every Roman did since Cicero, that Rome's second king, Numa, died long before Pythagoras was born; he also knew that the teachings which he crowded into this diatribe came from many different poetic and philosophical sources, not least the Sicilian Empedocles. But with it he accomplished two goals: to show that, far from being abnormal, metamorphosis was an essential process in the continued operation of the world and its inhabitants, and to reinforce the pattern of culture traveling west from Greece (or north from Magna Graecia) to Rome. One can add a third function: the recapitulation of themes from throughout the poem, especially its opening books.

"Pythagoras" opens by preaching abstention from animal flesh, arguing from the innocent nourishment of milk and honey and plants supplied by nature (cf. 1.112–3), from the vegetarian diet of domestic animals, and the fruits enjoyed by the golden age (15.97, cf. 1.104–6). An evil deity, whoever it might have been (the wording of 15.104 recalls the good deity of 1.32), taught men animal sacrifice, so that they behaved like wolves or Cyclopes, filling their flesh with the flesh of others (15.87–92). Like Lucretius, the prophet opens his denunciation of false religion by stressing the cruelty of sacrifice, the suffering of the victim, and the dishonesty of claiming this is pleasing to the gods.

In the next phase, Pythagoras claims inspiration by Apollo and echoes both Lucretius (1.926–30) and Virgil (*Georgics* 3.291–3) in his joy in knowledge, as he envisions soaring above men with pity for their folly and fear of death (15.143–52). In giving him this joyful pride, Ovid is signaling the self-consciously didactic nature of Pythagoras's teaching (Volk 2002: 64–7). But his message contradicts that of Lucretius: the soul is immortal and always moves from one body to another, just as he himself once lived as a Greek warrior at Troy. It is immune to death, and though all things change, nothing perishes, as the spirit flows from man to beast.

> As yielding wax is stamped with new designs
> And changes shape and seems not still the same,
> Yet is indeed the same, even so our souls
> Are still the same for ever, but adopt
> In their migrations ever varying forms. (15.169–72,
>   tr. Melville)

This protreptic section of Pythagoras's teaching ends as it began, with a prayer to refrain from the evil killing of souls which are our own kin. Does Ovid himself believe this? Or does he simply admire its idealism?

In the third section (176–236) the philosopher turns from ethics to cosmology. Nothing in the whole world abides, but everything flows (here Ovid echoes Heracleitus). Time itself glides like a river as day succeeds night, and dawn hands over the sky to Phoebus (189–92 might recall Phaethon, but now the sun is represented as a shield); the moon too waxes and wanes, and the seasons follow each other, imitating the ages of man. So spring is like a sucking baby, and summer a sturdy youth; autumn is a mature man, while aging winter comes with trembling step and balding gray hair (199–213). Human development, which has just served as a comparison, becomes the next focus, as Pythagoras traces the stages of our life from conception through growth to decay, and on to death. Though the soul survives, our body and human identity perish (214–36).

The elements too do not stay fixed, and Ovid recalls a number of these transformations from his cosmogony: their differential weight (15.242, cf. 1.30), the soaring of fire at first creation (15.248 ~.26) and the resolution of the elements as they re-form, fire thickening into air, air into earth, and earth into a ball of water (15.251 ~1.35). As he approaches the midpoint in the lecture, Pythagoras again couches natural change and renewal in the thematic language of metamorphosis:

> Nothing retains its form; new shapes from old
> Nature the great inventor ceaselessly
> Contrives. In all creation, be assured,
> There is no death—no death, but only change
> And innovation; what we men call birth
> Is but a different new beginning; death
> Is but to cease to be the same. (252–6, tr. Melville)

Pythagoras is moving from the abstractions of physics to the particulars of geology: seashells and anchors found inland, even on mountains, the ebb and flow of flood (recalling 1.281–92, 343–7), and shifting natural features. From now on, Ovid enriches the lecture with a mass of marvels known to us from other Greek and Roman writings. Tales of disappearing rivers (quoted by Seneca in his *Natural Questions*) and the drowned Peloponnesian cities Helice and Buris (already cited by Polybius and Strabo, recurring five times in Seneca, and in Pliny the Elder's *Natural History*) introduce strange accounts of the harmful properties of waters (a distinct topic in Pliny: although Seneca credits his ideas to Empedocles, he actually cites this speech four times as his authority). There are strategic echoes of earlier books: on the centaurs and Hercules (283–5, cf. 9.191); on the winds (298–303, recalling 1.56–8); and on the strange power of the spring Salmacis (319, cf. 4.285–7). Floating Delos and the clashing Symplegades (337–8) recall the adventures of Leto (6.333–6) and the Argonauts (7.1–7), while Etna evokes shipwrecked Achaemenides and his tale of the Cyclops (340–55; cf. 14.167–97).

At 356 the geographical catalogue yields to zoology: to the regeneration of bees (*bougonia*, 364–7, recalling Virgil's *Georgics* 4), chrysalises and tadpoles half-formed in mud (375–6 = 1.403–10, 428–9), and the she-bear's role in licking her newborn cubs into shape. The philosopher seems to stray from his argument to include delight in marvels like the peacock's tail (385, cf. 1.722–3) and the mythical self-renewing phoenix, which builds its own pyre, from which the newborn bird arises to carry its nest to the temple of the sun. Certainly, the miscellaneous notices of the sex-changing hyena and jewel-excreting lynx have wandered far from context.

Ovid has saved up the most important illustration of eternal change: the rise and fall of cities. In the second century B.C.E., both Greek and Near Eastern traditions (e.g., the seventh chapter of the Book of Daniel and the Hebrew-inspired fourth book of Sibylline oracles) knew the sequence of four empires—Assyria, Media, Persia, and Macedon—that had risen and declined, and were now adding to them the new rise of Rome. Did Ovid know Polybius's story (38.22) that Scipio Aemilianus looked on the ruins of conquered Carthage and quoted the lament of Hector for Troy in *Iliad* 6.448–9, foreseeing Rome's position in this sequence of empires? Given Pythagoras's date before the rise and fall of Persia and Macedon, Ovid substitutes a retrospect and prophecy based on Greek epic tradition. As Troy was once great in wealth and manpower, as Sparta and Mycenae flourished, and the Thebes of Oedipus and the Athens of Pandion, so Pythagoras heralds the rise of Rome by the waters of the Tiber and claims to recall the prophecy of Helenus to Aeneas— one that Helenus did not utter when they met in *Aeneid* 3. This is surely the climax of Pythagoras's diatribe, since it hails the future growth of Rome and the universal rule that a descendant of Iulus will confer upon it before he is taken to heaven (444–9). It might seem to follow from the whole extended argument that this too shall pass away, and Rome's empire will not be eternal, but no hint is given.

After his prophet's guarantee of the divinity of Caesar (or Augustus) and imperial Rome, the poet cuts away to his original message of metempsychosis and its moral implications. If human souls

can pass into living creatures, and domestic animals are our bene-
factors, let us not hunt or eat animal flesh. If we must kill predatory
creatures, let us be content to kill them and limit our mouths to innocent nourishment.

So this was Numa's education! It has been suggested that we are
supposed to find this lecture absurd, but there is no mockery of Numa
here or in other Augustan authors. He was the model king who in-
structed Rome in religion and the arts of peace. Might I suggest
instead that Ovid has colored with academic eccentricity a funda-
mentally well-conceived lecture, that the anecdotal marvels of 273–
417 are just a display of learning out of control? Perhaps one answer
is that the peculiar tales of cities swallowed up by nature and of animal regeneration complement and offset what might otherwise be
too solemn and moralizing a concentration on humanity and in particular on Rome and her destiny. As it is, Rome is only the last of
many cities named, and man is just one creature among insects, birds,
and beasts. As stimulus to the imagination this lecture offers a dazzling tour, reviving the miraculous aspect of the everyday while exciting the fancy with other, more fantastic wonders of the world.

Further Reading

On natural wonders, see K. S. Myers, *Ovid's Causes: Cosmology
and Aetiology in the Metamorphoses* (Ann Arbor, 1994); Stephen M.
Wheeler, *A Discourse of Wonders: Audience and Performance in Ovid's
"Metamorphoses"* (Philadelphia, 1999). On the Roman tradition of
didactic poetry reflected in the speech of Pythagoras, see K. Volk,
The Poetics of Latin Didactic: Lucretius, Vergil, Ovid, Manilius (Oxford,
2002), 64–7; and two important articles: P. R. Hardie, "The Speech
of Pythagoras in Ovid's *Metamorphoses* 15: Empedoclean Epos,"
Classical Quarterly 45 (1995): 204–14; and G. K. Galinsky, "The
Speech of Pythagoras at Ovid, *Metamorphoses* 15.75–478," *Papers of
the Leeds Latin Seminar* 10 (1998): 313–36.

· 9 ·

Genre and Narrative:
Ovid's Polymorphous Poem

When Ovid was a young man, Rome's dean of poets, Horace, wrote a poem that styled itself as a letter of literary advice to the young sons of the aristocrat Piso. By the time of Quintilian, around 90 C.E., this was already known as *Ars poetica* (Art of poetry). In it Horace sketches rapidly the origin of the classical Greek verse genres associated with different meters, from elegy, couched in the elegiac couplet of inscriptions (hexameters alternating with shorter, end-stopped pentameters), to the dialogue of comedy and tragedy set in the iambic trimeter coined for satirical invective by Archilochus. But although Horace was himself writing in (a slightly freer version of) the hexameters that Ovid would use for *Metamorphoses,* he says nothing of the generic and stylistic range of hexameter poetry, perhaps just because he is treating it as a basic, or default, meter. The dactylic hexameter was the meter of the earliest known poetry—of oracles, of Homer's epics, of Hesiod, and after him of genealogical and didactic poetry. But while dramatic meters were mostly confined to the stage, both the hexameter and the elegiac couplet came to be used for an increasing variety of writings—new genres (if genres are defined by content, tone, and style). Horace followed Lucilius in using the hexameter for satirical comments and anecdotes about the world around him and for the personal moral reflections of his *Epistles,* shaped according to their different addressees. Virgil wrote only in hexameters, developing minor variations of technique from his early pastoral songs and poems about song to his didactic *Georgics,* instructing and encouraging the farmer, and his mature national epic.

But after the poetry that formed the culture of classical Athens, the new society created by the Hellenistic empires produced a new poetry, self-consciously different from the classical genres. At Alexandria, Theocritus wrote pastoral and urban poetry in hexameters; Apollonius composed his epic voyage of the Argonauts, an epic colored by the legacy of Euripidean tragedy as well as Homer; and others, such as Aratus and Nicander, produced didactic poems on astronomy, medicine, and botany. The most versatile of these learned cosmopolitan poets was Callimachus, who adapted elegiac couplets to retelling stories of city foundations and the origins of names and customs from all over Greece, freely choosing and changing his versions of other men's myths. Although Callimachus also wrote personal epigrams of love, friendship, and criticism, he was most influential through his less personal elegy, in which irony, detachment, allusiveness, and variety of tone and pace together constituted a distinctive idiom. He also wrote at least one short narrative in hexameters, the *Hecale,* which countered epic content—the hero Theseus setting out to fight the monstrous bull of Marathon, and the establishment of an Athenian festival—with the calculated simplicity of Hecale's hospitality to the hero when he was forced to shelter from the storm in her hut.

Two generations before Ovid, Catullus and his friends adopted Callimachean principles, translating some of his poetry and imitating his techniques in a new kind of hexameter poem. Only Catullus 64 survives, celebrating the wedding of Peleus and Thetis with the embedded internal narrative of Ariadne abandoned on Naxos. His friend Cinna composed a miniature epic on Myrrha's incestuous passion, and Calvus told the story of Io's rape by Jupiter. (The short epic called *Ciris,* on Scylla's criminal passion for Minos, seems to be dependent on Ovid.) Other miniature epics (of unknown authorship) reflect the influence of *Hecale,* such as *Culex,* the pathetic tale of the gnat crushed when he saved a shepherd from a deadly snake, and *Moretum,* a realistic portrait of a peasant rising to light his fire and prepare his lunch. By the time Virgil composed the sixth *Eclogue,* the song he created for Silenus shows that the poet knew or could imagine almost every kind of poetry in hexameters, from cosmogony, to erotic myth, to tales of metamorphosis, and poems celebrating the artistic succession handed down from Orpheus and Hesiod to Virgil's older friend Gallus.

Ovid's own career brought him to narrative hexameter poetry after more than twenty years as a successful composer of love elegy, first "autobiographical," then mythical and even didactic. Didactic poetry was normally composed in hexameters (like Lucretius's *On Nature* and Virgil's *Georgics*), but Ovid had continued to use elegiac verse for his three books of instruction to lovers and one professing to provide remedies for love. He even composed a tragedy, the *Medea.* Ovid may also have begun his new elegiac sequence called *Fasti,* which celebrated the festivals and myths of the Roman calendar, soon after he embarked on the *Metamorphoses.* Familiarity with the ideals of Callimachus had encouraged Roman poets to fuse different types of narrative and levels of seriousness within single works or collections, until, like the menus of cosmopolitan cuisine, the diet stimulated the reader with the piquancy of the hybrid and the unexpected.

We saw that the *Metamorphoses* opens with the poet's assertion of his independent pursuit of novelty. But the expectation of epic set up by Ovid's meter would not be disturbed by the opening cosmogony and portrayal of the golden age. The council of the gods was another epic feature of the *Iliad, Odyssey,* and *Aeneid.* But then this council invites a second level of reading. This Jupiter is more angry than just, and the gods clearly fear to offend him. Jupiter makes himself the sole witness of what he claims is a monstrous conspiracy among men and of an attempt on his life by Lycaon, which he has already punished. But he is not content with this: humanity must be eliminated before it infects the world. In the circumstances, the comparison of Olympus with the Augustan Palatine does more to demean Jupiter and his yes-gods than exalt Augustus. Ovid provides a grandiose flood, but the demigods involved, such as Boreas and Triton, are too fanciful to be convincing, and the paradoxes of the flood, as seals are caught in treetops and wolves swim for their lives alongside lambs, counteract the awe it might otherwise provoke. Even Ovid's originality and symmetry of expression, reversing the increase of the waters by their decrease, teases with a formal patterning that cancels emotional involvement. But despite his skillful distancing of emotion, Ovid will not allow the listener or reader to relax and enjoy the narrative like a satirical novel: the new act of creation by Deucalion and Pyrrha leads to highly imaginative, quasi-Lucretian accounts of the genesis of life and the hazards of misformed creatures.

With the monstrous Python, killed by Apollo as his first heroic feat, one might anticipate a return to grand divine narrative and the foundation of the Delphic oracle, as lovers of Greek poetry would remember from the Homeric and Callimachean hymns to Apollo. Instead, Ovid prefers the love stories passed over by "Homer" and confronts his audience with a new beginning (1.452–3): "Apollo's first love was Daphne, Peneus's daughter. This was not caused by unwitting chance but by Cupid's savage anger." Talk of the god's first love suggests that there will be other love stories (there will); the trigger of Cupid's savage anger would instantly recall the savage anger of Juno that persecuted the first man to come from Troy. The tale unfolds as Cupid, angered by Apollo's taunt that his brother is too young to play with real heroic weapons, turns his bow against Apollo and wounds him through the heart. Again the audience would recall how Ovid himself was wounded through the heart by Cupid in the opening poem of his elegiac *Amores* and became lovesick but was rapidly provided by Cupid with an accommodating girl as the object of his poems and attentions (*Amores* 1, *Elegies* 1, 2, and 3). In *Metamorphoses* Cupid spitefully complements his first shot with a second, of a lead-tipped arrow that turns away from love, so that Apollo is smitten with love for Daphne, who has just been inoculated with aversion. His address to Daphne is in familiar elegiac terms and might seem a reasonably acceptable form of wooing if she were not already in flight. The situation is designed to produce elegiac paradigms of behavior but then disappoint them. When Daphne rejects his plea to run more slowly, Apollo turns from persuasion to contemplate force. By the time her transformation into a laurel tree puts her beyond his reach, the reader is no longer willing to accept his promise to honor her branches in Roman triumphs, or as ornaments for the doorway of Augustus, as fair compensation. The compliment to the princeps is undercut by the foolishness of the young god—Augustus's patron god at that.

Readers who had enjoyed Ovid's earlier work were no doubt relieved to meet the familiar sentimentality of elegy but then disturbed to find the episode transforming as it evolved. It is not only Ovid's characters but his stories that metamorphose, like Arachne's web, with "subtle, delicate tints / that change insensibly from shade to shade, so when the sunshine strikes a shower of rain / the bow's huge arc will paint the whole wide sky / and countless different colours shine" (6.62–6, tr. Melville). And they shift through all the generic colors. The most frequent and recognizable counterweight to epic grandeur in this composite poem is surely the world of elegy: *amor* outweighs *arma,* and women have a most undesirable prominence. As elegy thrived on the jealousy, frustration, and separation of lovers, and the contemplation of death, so Ovid selects myths that provoke such emotions.

But some love is too easily satisfied to be elegiac. Jupiter can consummate whatever desire takes him, and Mercury meets no serious rejection; the latter's sexual adventures are nearer comedy than elegy. But when Mercury prinks himself and straightens his cloak before going to find his beloved Herse, he is following Ovid's prescription for the elegiac suitor in the *Art of Love.* Nor do all lovers earn readers' sympathy: even selfish Narcissus derives his thoughts and actions from his role as lover—if only of himself. In his *furor,* or sick passion, his long unanswered appeals take the form of pleas to a distant beloved and culminate in the romantic notion of sharing death together, an elegiac extravagance which provides the climax

of the tale of Pyramus and Thisbe in book 4 and of Ceyx and Alcyone in book 11 (the shared death and transfiguration of Baucis
and Philemon depend on the same tender sentiments).

Gods cannot die, and cannot weep, as Ovid reports (2.621–2) at
the death of Apollo's faithless beloved, Coronis. But they can lament, and lament is a fundamental mode of elegy that goes back to
the myth of Orpheus. Yet critics have differed in reading his pleas
to the lords of the dead (10.17–39) as unrelieved pathos or as rhetorical overkill, calculated to distance sympathy. On his return Orpheus
adopts his professional persona to present a song program colored
by his eroticism. As the first poet, he should have sung an epic lay
about the first great conflict between gods and giants, but Ovid exploits his own predecessors and makes the fact that Orpheus sang of
such things in Apollonius's epic an excuse to limit his current
themes to "boys beloved of the gods" and "girls struck by illicit passion duly punished for their lust" (10.148–54). So his lay begins and
ends with elegiac material: the love of a god for a mortal and lament
for his death. It is elegiac that both Apollo and Venus desert their
cult sites to be with their beloved and humble themselves as hunting companions; that Hyacinthus causes his own death by rushing
to catch Apollo's discus; that Adonis, whose beauty Ovid compares
with Cupid himself, incurs his fatal wound by neglecting Venus's
warning and hunting a savage boar. When Orpheus's father, Apollo,
apostrophizes Hyacinthus, reproaching himself for his death, he
utters a lament that echoes Virgil's account of the first lament of
Orpheus (*Georgics* 4.464–6) and that is constructed around pathetic
reiteration of "you": "you will always be with me and stay on my
unforgetting lips; it is you whom the lyre struck by my hand and our
poems will celebrate." Orpheus may be an oral bard but Ovid is a
textual poet, so his Apollo presents the writing of a text as Hyacinthus's best memorial, inscribing his groans AIAI on its leaves, so
that the flower bears this inscription (10.215–6; see p. 78). And lest the
readers should forget Orpheus's self-imposed choice of "the lighter
lyre" or Ovid's Greek erudition, his last words are an etymology:
Adonis's flower is called "anemone" because the winds (*anemoi*) blow
it away, "quick to fall because of its lightness" (737–8).

Besides elegiac sentimentality it may be useful to distinguish three other recurring modes, without treating them as mutually exclusive or ignoring their occasional coincidence. Indeed, whether the primary tone of a narrative is solemn, comic, or ironic, elegy is always within reach, simply by adding brushstrokes of elegiac diction, like "endearments" (*blanditiae*), "girlfriend" (*puella*), or "mistress" (*domina*). Ovid's control of vocabulary and sentence structure can produce instant or gradual shifts of tone. What I have called the solemn mode is not a parody but is to some extent a conscious role-playing, as Ovid applies the traditional patterns of epic. In his Medea narrative, when the dragon must be put to sleep (7.149–58), Ovid constructs long complex periodic sentences, using formal relative clauses, anaphora (7.155), poetic compound adjectives like *pervigil* and *praesignis* (ever-watchful, most-conspicuous), periphrases like *Aesonius heros* (the hero born of Aeson), wordplay such as the allusion to Medea as *spolia altera* ("secondary spoils"; cf. 13.624), and assonance (on *a* and *r* in 7.151, on *i, c,* and *o* in 7.158). There are similar extended and enriched passages at 7.179–87 (Medea's night magic), 9.229–38 (where Ovid apostrophizes the transfigured Hercules), 13.632–9 (Anius's temple ritual), and 14.845–51 (the deification of Romulus's wife, Hersilia). Most of these high-epic passages are short, perhaps because Ovid has difficulty restraining his humor and irony. Certainly, just as he can raise his tone with grandiose compounds, so he can bring the reader down to earth with prosaic words and images, most famously when he compares the blood gushing from Pyramus's wound to water from a burst pipe (4.121–4).

A favorite contrast with the epic mode comes from the humor of trickery, imitating not specific ancient genres but actions and attitudes common to comedy and mime. Deception in a trivial cause such as seduction is its essence. Thus, we would probably deny the name of comedy to Mercury's killing of Argos, as Ovid implies by his melancholy apostrophe "you lie dead, Argos, and the light you had in so many orbs of light is quenched, while a single night has possessed a hundred eyes" (1.720–1). But Mercury's trick on the dishonest Battus is pure comedy, as he returns in disguise to bribe the old man to break his promise. Disguise is a favorite theme of comedy, and so gods and shape-shifters, with their control over metamorphosis, usually bring comedy: witness Vertumnus, who dresses as an old woman to woo Pomona for himself, or Mnestra, the shapeshifting daughter of bankrupt Erysichthon (8.846–74), who takes a new shape each time that she is sold and escapes from each master in turn. More complex is Ovid's play with irony. Irony is not a genre, but it is perhaps the best single term for the mode of Ovid's oblique and shifting Callimachean narratives. An early example is the sequence in book 2 adapted from Callimachus's *Hecale,* where Ovid glides from the new plumage of Juno's peacock to the tale of how the raven (Apollo's sacred bird) lost her whiteness as punishment for informing on Coronis's infidelity. The raven is intercepted in midflight by a crow (2.547), who buttonholes him with her life story: she too was once beautiful, indeed a princess, until she angered her patron goddess Minerva. This conversation between birds, which survives in fragmentary form in *Hecale,* is quite alien to previous epics. Each tale leads back and away from its starting point, so that the story of the daughters of Cecrops is suspended until we hear how Minerva saved the princess from rape by turning her into a crow. Undeterred, the raven completes his destructive mission, driving Apollo to kill his pregnant beloved, whereupon he grieves over her corpse but saves her child.

This child, Aesculapius, becomes the new focus as he is fostered by the centaur Chiron, and Chiron's daughter Ocyroe foretells his second escape from death—and is punished, like the birds, for telling what should be kept secret. As she describes her gradual transformation into a mare, Ovid diverts us with her protest, "Why should I become completely horse? My father has both horse and human shape." Why indeed? The unanswered question momentarily preoccupies the reader; what was she before?

But the story has taken off again, and its rapid pace is part of the mechanism that prevents emotional engagement. Chiron begs Apollo for help, but Apollo cannot disobey Jove—and anyway he is out of earshot, playing shepherd and sounding the panpipes obsessed by love (2.676–83). It is up to the reader to remember the story of Apollo's service as shepherd to King Admetus, before Mercury seizes the chance to rustle Apollo's unguarded cattle, which leads to the tale of Battus, turned by Mercury into a stone that still marks the spot.

As Mercury approaches Athens, the devotee of Callimachus would have recognized lines echoing a local reference from *Hecale* (2.709–10). Mercury spots Herse as he flies overhead and primps himself before approaching the home of the three daughters of Cecrops. Aglauros intercepts him and, like Battus, plans to cheat him of his request. Now Ovid reminds the reader of Aglauros's intrusion on Minerva's secret (748–9 recalls 560–1), as she demands gold from Mercury and sends him away. Pallas, who punished the crow by withdrawing her favor, sees Aglauros's behavior and sends Jealousy to torment her. (Here Ovid indulges in the double ekphrasis, or descriptive set-piece, discussed in ch. 8.) Readers will never know the outcome of Mercury's interest in Herse, but when Aglauros bars the door, he turns her—again like Battus—to stone on the spot, its livid color a lasting witness to her jealousy.

Only some of these linked stories come from the single context in Callimachus, and even so, the main motif of his *Hecale* is reserved for book 8, where Theseus is intercepted by Achelous and subjected to his host's tales of past misfortune. Achelous's hospitality is far from Hecale's humble fare, but Ovid reserves that theme for a tale he has inserted into the after-dinner conversation—the hospitality of Baucis and Philemon.

In what spirit do readers or listeners accept and follow—if they can—this chain of stories of malice and indiscretion punished? Perhaps the birds set the tone, directing listeners to hear their tales as Aesopian fables. Nowhere else in the *Metamorphoses* do transformed humans act and talk in their animal form. Some of this is comic, but the melodramatic fates of Ocyroe and Aglauros invite a moral reaction.

Much of the elusive tone of this sequence has been contributed by successive narrators. Ovid makes brilliant play with "unreliable" narrators, starting with Jupiter himself. We also meet in this first book the recycling of a story by Mercury, whose protracted narrative of Pan and Syrinx (echoing Apollo and Daphne) bores Argos to sleep but does not prevent the poet intervening in person to complete the tale. Book 5 contains the celebrated doubly embedded narrative in which a Muse repeats to Pallas Athene Calliope's epic tale of Persephone and, within this mini-epic, the triply embedded narrative in which the Muse repeats Calliope's formal introduction of Arethusa's narrative of her narrow escape from rape by Achelous. Cephalus in book 7 has good reason to offer a different, self-exonerating version of his troubled and finally fatal marriage to Procris.

In his fall of Troy in books 12–13, Ovid resorts both to internal narrators and to a multigeneric sequence. Rather than compete with Homer by reprising his epic narrative, Ovid substitutes episodes taken from other genres. For the *Iliad,* he substitutes Achilles' earlier combat with the superhuman Cycnus, Nestor's rambling account of the wedding brawl of the Lapiths and centaurs, a full-length rhetorical *agon* of Ajax and Ulysses competing for dead Achilles' armor (13.1–398), and the core of a Euripidean tragedy, *Hecuba.* From this tragic action Ovid adapts the messenger speech and Hecuba's lament for her children, then converts and compresses the dramatic catastrophe into an epic narrative. To all this he attaches a sort of epilogue deliberately recalling the supplication of Achilles' mother, Thetis, in the *Iliad,* where Memnon's divine mother successfully appeals to Jupiter for honors to her dead son.

For his alternative version of Virgil's *Aeneid* 2–3, Ovid brings the Trojans swiftly to the Straits of Messina, then diverts his readers with a number of local excursions. When Aeneas reaches Sicily, primed with Helenus's directions (13.722–4), the mention of Scylla, the local hazard, sends the narrative looping back to old cautionary tales. Ovid goes back to the time when Scylla is not yet a sea monster but a beautiful nymph who boasts of the young lovers she has deceived. Like the raven princess, she is warned in vain by one of her own kind, the nymph Galatea, who tells of her own loss as Scylla combs Galatea's hair.

The tale of Galatea is the remarkable love triangle involving her beloved Acis and the unwelcome suitor Polyphemus. Acis has no previous literary existence, though he has a future in Handel's splendid opera. Galatea, whom Raphael will immortalize in the wonderful wall-painting of the Farnesina, has appeared only once before in classical poetry, as the silent and uncooperative sea nymph wooed in vain by Theocritus's young Cyclops in *Idyll* 6. There the Cyclops is a clumsy and lovesick but harmless shepherd, who bravely accepts his single eye and his hairy features. So, when Galatea begins, Ovid's audience may have expected a retelling of Theocritus. But there are significant differences. Ovid's Galatea has a handsome boy lover, in whose lap she lies cuddled in her grotto. And his Cyclops is a dreadful figure, making inanimate nature shudder in revulsion, ruthless to strangers, and contemptuous of the gods. But now he has been struck by love, he is indifferent to his sheep and cave home. Like Mercury, or Theocritus's young Cyclops, Polyphemus, for it is he, tries to make himself smart, combing his stiff hair with a rake and shaving with a scythe (there is a vivid second-century mosaic in Cordova that shows Galatea turning away to her pet sea serpent as the Cyclops woos her, holding a huge lopsided rake). Ovid marks him as the bloodthirsty Polyphemus of the *Odyssey* but rewrites the authentic Homeric warning: Polyphemus boasts that when he was warned by the prophet Telemus that his eye would be stolen from him, he only laughed, claiming "another has already stolen it" (13.768–78).

Ovid concentrates his parodic skills in the pseudopastoral song of Polyphemus (13.789–869). It starts with the comparative sequence of Theocritus's love song ("O ruddier than the cherry . . ."), but both the positive images of Galatea's beauty and the negative symbols of her cruelty run to excess, culminating in the triple comparison of her speed in flight with deer, wind, and breeze, and a sinister threat ("if you only knew, you would curse your delaying and strive to keep me"). Like Theocritus's young shepherd, the ogre proudly describes his assets of cool grotto and rich fruit from every kind of tree, his flock beyond counting and abundant milk and cheese. He has love gifts of does and pigeons and twin bear cubs, which he has kept "for my mistress!" (how soon will they be as shaggy and ungovernable as he is?). The ogre even praises his hairiness and compares his hideous single eye to a great shield, an orb equal to the sun itself. Like an ordinary suitor, he boasts of his high birth, from the sea god, and belittles Jupiter.

So far the song seems to be pastoral-comical-elegiac. What breaks the illusion is the fury of his jealousy at the thought of Acis and his violent threats to tear the boy limb from limb and scatter his body over the waters, as he burns with a passion that makes him feel a veritable Aetna.

But is this song comic? The ogre's mounting frenzy moves from incongruous adoration of the Nereid and fear of her anger to an outburst of rage at the name of Acis. As Joseph Farrell (1992) has shown, this is the brutal Cyclops of the *Odyssey* and *Aeneid,* inflamed with an arrogance that despises Olympus and who compares himself with the sun or a great shield like that of Achilles that stands for the world itself. The voice of pastoral is overlaid with epic through Ovid's allusions not only to Homer but to two Virgilian adaptations: the lovesick shepherd Corydon of *Eclogue* 2 and the Cyclops of *Aeneid* 3. It is this brute who gets the upper hand in the battle of genres, culminating in murder as he crushes the fleeing boy Acis with a great lump torn from the mountain (13.883). When Odysseus blinded him, the Cyclops missed his aim and the ship escaped, but Ovid's Ulysses is still to come. Luckily, Galatea uses her grandfather Nereus's powers to give Acis new life, and he emerges as a noble river, taller than before and most magnificently blue.

Ovid has not forgotten Scylla and uses a similar motif, the transformation of a new blue sea god, to bring on the ex-fisherman Glaucus as her suitor. Her rejection takes him to Circe, whose jealousy when Glaucus spurns her leads her to infect Scylla's bathing pool and disfigure her rival with a girdle of yapping dogs (14.25–67). Finally, we are back to Scylla, point of departure in 13.730.

In some respects this chain of lovers' spite echoes the Callimachean chain of stories in the second half of book 2. And parts of this sequence not only are Callimachean in manner but must surely derive from that poet's lost work, *Glaucus*. We do not know whether Ovid or Callimachus originated the striking first-person reminiscences of Ovid's narrative. Glaucus tells "how I became a god" (13.930–57). Hippolytus, now renamed Virbius, as his Italic second self, offers an unparalleled report of "how I was fatally wounded by my horses" (15.506–29) in a myth that we know Callimachus included in his *Aitia*.

It seems, then, that Ovid can weave a chain of iridescent tales out of one or more preexisting texts, using material from different genres or grafting threads drawn from his own imagination with equal ease. To change the image, the *Metamorphoses* and its many narratives are like a complex necklace whose central strand sustains loops (both short and long) of beads of different colors and materials, which separate and rejoin the main ordered sequence at different places to create an overall symmetry. I have singled out from this epic sequence arabesques of pathetic (elegiac), comic, ironic, and multivoiced narratives, but there is no comprehensive account that will do equal justice to Ovid's shifting tones, his generic play, and his gift for evoking the most memorable phrases and moments of each and every Greek and Roman poetic tradition.

Further Reading

On Ovidian narrators and narrative, see Joseph B. Solodow, *The World of Ovid's "Metamorphoses"* (Chapel Hill, 1988), chs. 2, 4, and 5. On elegiac elements in the *Metamorphoses,* see P. E. Knox, *Ovid's Metamorphoses and the Tradition of Augustan Poetry,* Proceedings of the Cambridge Philological Society, Suppl. 11 (Cambridge, 1986); S. E. Hinds, *The Metamorphosis of Persephone* (Cambridge, 1988); A. Barchiesi, "Narrative Technique and Narratology in the *Metamorphoses*," in *The Cambridge Companion to Ovid,* ed. P. R. Hardie (Cambridge, 2002). On book 2, see A. M. Keith, *The Play of Fictions: Studies in Ovid's "Metamorphoses" Book 2* (Ann Arbor, 1992). On Ovid's "little *Aeneid*," see G. Tissol, *The Face of Nature: Wit, Narrative, and Cosmic Origins in Ovid's "Metamorphoses"* (Princeton, 1997).

On Cephalus, see R. J. Tarrant, "The Silence of Cephalus: Text and Narrative Technique in Ovid," *Transactions of the American Philological Association* 125 (1995): 99–111. On Polyphemus, see J. Farrell, "Dialogues of Genre in Ovid's 'Love-Song of Polyphemus,'" *American Journal of Philology* 113 (1992): 235–68. On the elegiac Apollo in books 1 and 10, see John F. Miller, "The Lamentations of Apollo in Ovid's *Metamorphoses*," in *Ovid: Werk und Wirkung. Festgabe . . . von Albrecht* (Frankfurt, 1999), 413–21.

·10·

After Ovid

Ovid was famous and successful before he began the *Metamorphoses*, but it is probable that in the two millennia after his death his epic of transformation not only transformed epic but exercised a greater influence over the shaping of art and literature than any other Latin work. Anyone attempting to convey the breadth and variety of this influence can only pick a small sample of works that have themselves been the subject of many books. To provide some perspective this chapter will begin and end with popular art forms from the last decade.

Like many others I saw *Metamorphoses* in New York in 2002: this was the stage presentation by Mary Zimmerman of about a dozen episodes from Ovid, enhanced by Apuleius's tale of Cupid and Psyche and Rilke's poetic evocation of the dead Eurydice's indifference to her past life and love. Zimmerman chose as setting a large shallow pool surrounded by a boardwalk and distributed the parts of narrator, gods, and mortals among about a dozen players, who alternated speech and dumb-show to enact the tales. The use of the pool had provoked a momentary hope that we might be shown Salmacis and Hermaphroditus, but naturally only episodes were chosen which did not require a scenically impossible transformation. The shipwreck and drowning of Ceyx and his final watery reunion with Alcyone could be fully represented; even Narcissus was given a minute of silent self-adoration at the poolside before he was bodily removed and replaced by a potted plant. In general, Zimmerman concentrated on love stories and alternated tragic and humorous episodes, but the scenes began and ended with the fate of the same character, Midas.

Thus, Ceyx and Alycone, Orpheus and Eurydice, and somewhat boldly Myrrha and her father, Cinyras, represented the tragic side of love; comedy was supplied by the autophagy of Erysichthon, a totally remodeled scene of Phaethon explaining his problematic relationship with his father to a therapist after the crash, and the bustling hospitality of Philemon and Baucis to the gods Jupiter and Mercury, with their reward of simultaneous transformation into trees. The descent of the gods from their elevated perch down to the stage at mortal level, and the couple's mutual farewell, pointed toward closure, sealed by the ring-composition of Midas's final return from his quest to put right the harm his golden touch had done—but more of that below.

The Visual Tradition

A ncient artists knew that you could not represent process but only the moment before or after transformation. Thus, on Greek vases Peleus and Thetis wrestle in human form, surrounded by images of Thetis's other animal shapes, and it is an exception that the Tyrrhenian pirates dive from their ship with human lower limbs and dolphin heads and breasts. The same decorum was observed for depicting Ovidian metamorphosis during the golden period of European art, which bloomed in the sixteenth century. We might start with some brilliant but isolated works: the mysterious scene painted by Piero di Cosimo variously known as *The Death of Procris* and *Satyr Mourning Over a Nymph* (figure 1) and *The Fall of Icarus* by Peter Bruegel (figure 2). Each depicts a moment following the catastrophe of Ovid's tale. Procris lies dead upon a bare headland, with the spires of a distant city across the bay; most prominent is the dog Laelaps, which keeps a melancholy watch at her side (Piero was sentimental; he also puts the *Liebestod* of the centaurs Cyllarus and Hylonome in the foreground of his *Battle of Lapiths and Centaurs;* like his *Procris,* this is in London's National Gallery). In the lovely Bruegel land and seascape, the plowman, shepherd, and fisherman of *Metamorphoses* 8.217–18 are too busy at their tasks to notice the splash of the boy Icarus's body just sinking beneath the calm waters.

In Italy at this time Raphael's pupil Giulio Romano was decorating the Palazzo del Té, summer residence of the dukes of Mantua, with a Sala di Ovidio and other Ovidian rooms: the Sala dei Giganti depicted the fall of the giants thunderstruck by Jupiter (*Met.* 1.152–5) and a smaller chamber featured the disaster of Phaethon's fall and scenes from both Ovid's and Apuleius's *Metamorphoses,* including a Polyphemus with Acis and Galatea.

Titian's most famous mythological paintings are probably his Bacchus and Ariadne (London, National Gallery, Venice Cat. no. 3), based not on *Metamorphoses* but on book 1 of the *Art of Love,* and the sensual Danae (Naples, Capodimonte, Cat. 40), again, Ovidian in spirit but not based on *Metamorphoses.* But as an older man after 1550 we find him composing Ovidian *Poesie,* including Diana and Actaeon (figure 3). One version, with its companion piece Diana and Callisto, is in Edinburgh (Hardie CC. figs. 1 and 2); the other, showing Actaeon already transformed and assailed by his hounds, is in the National Gallery, London (Hardie CC. fig. 6). Among his other representations of scenes from the *Metamorphoses* is the *Rape of Europa* (Boston, Gardner Museum, Barkan 1990: no. 29), but the strapping lass is spread-eagled across the divine bull's back in a most un-Ovidian posture. If it was a mark of Renaissance decorum that "the integrity and dignity of the human body are to be preserved" (Allen 2002: 341), Titian has given himself amazing license. He also painted Perseus and Andromeda (London, Wallace Colln. Barkan 1990: no. 32), Venus trying to dissuade Adonis from the hunt (twice; see Venice Cat. 5 and 60), and a grim punishment of Marsyas now in Lichtenstein (Cat. 76) in which Apollo, holding his viol, observes the satyr hung and flayed in ugly shades of brown and purple (some

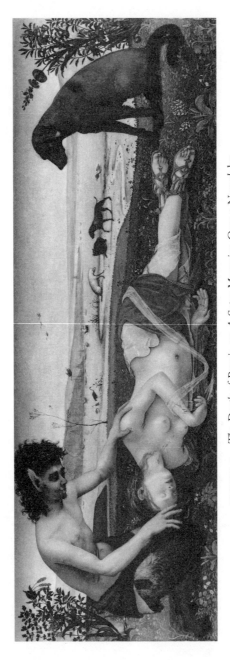

FIGURE 1 *The Death of Procris,* or *A Satyr Mourning Over a Nymph* by Piero di Cosimo. Used by permission of the National Gallery of London.

FIGURE 2 *The Fall of Icarus* by Pieter Brueghel. Used
by permission of the Royal Museum of Fine Arts,
Brussels, Belgium.

scholars see this as a very late work of the aging artist; others deny
its authenticity).

Among the many Italian, French, and Flemish artists who took
up these themes after Titian, Poussin deserves special mention. To
quote Anthony Blunt:

> His favorite source is Ovid's *Metamorphoses,* and his themes
> are the loves of gods which are recounted there: Venus with
> Mars, Adonis or Mercury; Diana and Endymion; Apollo
> and Daphne; Mercury and Herse; Echo and Narcissus; Ceph-
> alus and Aurora. The theme of love is a steady undercurrent
> to all the paintings of the 1630's, but they are the reverse of
> erotic. They are indeed rather elegiac, and the burden of
> Poussin's song is the unhappiness of love, rather than its
> physical charms. (Blunt 1967: no. 163)

FIGURE 3 *Diana and Actaeon* by Titian. From the Duke
of Sutherland Collection, on loan to the National Gallery
of Scotland.

Of Poussin's many Ovidian scenes we might note several exquisite
landscapes which dwarf the human figures: not only the two versions in which a huge Polyphemus looms over the embracing Acis
and Galatea (figure 4) (Blunt 1967: nos. 31 [= Hardie 2002: no. 5],
= Blunt 190) but also a Pyramus and Thisbe (Blunt 1967: no. 187), a
Juno, Io, and Argus (Blunt 1967: no. 97), and a Herse, Mercury, and
Aglauros (Blunt 1967: no. 19). As a landscape artist Poussin preferred images dominated by natural scenery, but some paintings,
such as the pathetic Echo, half-hidden as she looks down on the re-
cumbent Narcissus (Blunt 1967: no. 28), or Phaethon imploring Sol
(no. 69) or Pan and Syrinx (no. 107), are centered on the figures of

FIGURE 4   *Acis and Galatea* by Nicolas Poussin. Used by
permission of the National Gallery of Ireland.

the drama. Both his painted versions of Apollo and Daphne (nos. 32
and 251) show Daphne undergoing change, and one foregrounds
her with her arms already turned to branches, but no painting has
the virtuosity or passion of Bernini's sculptural masterpiece in the
Villa Borghese (Hardie 2002: fig. 4). Only Bernini's earlier *Rape of
Persephone* (also in the Villa Borghese) even approaches the frozen
movement of Daphne in flight.

The generation of di Cosimo and Romano coincided with the
first age of print, and of illustrated texts of and about *Metamorphoses.* A new wide-ranging study by Marina Warner, *Fantastic Metamorphoses, Other Worlds: Ways of Telling the Self* (Oxford 2002) illustrates vivid vignettes of metamorphosis in process from *Ovide Moralisé*
(*La Bible des Poètes*: figures 1, 2, and a comical Picus transformed
in plate 4) and samples later representations of Arachne "already
half-spider" (figure 3, from Doré's version of Dante *Purgatorio* 12),
Tithonus, Glaucus, and Io (figures 5, 7, 9). But Ovid is only Warner's

starting point for exploration of ethnographical and fictional texts interpreting the beliefs of other worlds and times about mutations of the self. Thus she leads from the running theme of Arachne's humiliation "on the ragged remnants of work that you had wrought to your own hurt" (*Purgatorio* 12, 44–45, tr. Mandelbaum) to the work of two great modern allegorists, Kafka portraying Gregor Samsa degraded into a cockroach, and Nabokov, both novelist and lepidopterist, describing empathetically the moments of natural change in the cycle from grub to butterfly, and deploying it in his fiction as a poignant symbol to contrast with human death (113–18).

The Literary Tradition

The urge to re-present and to emulate Ovid's scenes may have begun early; Seneca calls upon Ovid's flood to illustrate cataclysm in his *Natural Questions* (3.28–9), and Apuleius devotes a brilliant verbal description (ekphrasis) to a marble statue of Diana in a grotto sculpted to represent her vengeance on Actaeon in *Metamorphoses* 2.4. The poet Statius created his own Ovidian myth of a naiad in flight from Pan as a compliment to his patron Atedius Melior's sloping plane tree (*Silvae* 2.3), and two centuries later Claudian echoed the style and spirit of Ovid in his independent retelling, *The Rape of Proserpina.*

In the Middle Ages, those who could read learnt by reading Latin, and if the end of their studies was the Vulgate, Ovid lay well within their understanding: learned men composed *accessus* (introductions) to the *Metamorphoses,* especially to draw analogies between Ovid's creation and that of Genesis. It was perhaps inevitable that Ovid's text would be distorted to provide a series of morals, and the huge versified *Ovide moralisé,* followed by Pierre Bersuire's Latin commentary, dominated the outlook of the fourteenth century. Thus, Daedalus was explained as a sinner escaping from the devil Minos, or alternatively God himself, with Icarus representing a Christian worshiper; Daphne was a virgin fleeing corruption (fair enough!) or else the blessed Virgin Mary herself, but then so was

Myrrha (impregnated as she was by the Father); Alcyone was the Christian soul and her beloved Ceyx was Christ. Christine de Pizan (*Livre de la cité des dames*) saw Ovid as an evil corrupter, who was first exiled, then castrated for his offenses.

Chaucer at least resisted this allegorization, and loved Ovidian narrative for itself. His earliest work, the *Book of the Duchess,* exploited the world of sleep and dreams to retell the romantic tragedy of Alcyone and Ceyx, diverging from Ovid chiefly in avoiding the final transformation; Alcyone simply dies on the third day after her vision. Another of Chaucer's works, *The Legend of Good Women,* dwells chiefly on the deserted heroines of Ovid's *Heroides,* but it also celebrates Thisbe and Philomela, showing Chaucer's familiarity with Ovid by inserting into his tale of Theseus and Ariadne a brief report of Scylla's murder of her father, Nisus—again without any hint of Ovid's transformation. *The House of Fame* explores the implications of Ovid's allegorization in *Metamorphoses* 12: in the first book Chaucer reports that he dreamed of a temple of Venus inscribed with the narrative of *Aeneid* 1–4, then calls on Ovid's Dido from *Heroides* 7 to refute the Virgilian version of her guilt ("O how a woman doth amis / to love him that unknowen is"); in the second book he dreams that Jupiter has sent his eagle to display and interpret the House of Fame, her palace "betwixen hevene, erthe and see" to which all speech soars, both "fals" and "soth." The notion of soaring leads to references not only to Scipio's dream in Cicero but to Daedalus, Phaethon, and the constellations reported in *Metamorphoses* and other works. The *Canterbury Tales* too use the *Metamorphoses* for the Manciple's tale of Apollo's crow (actually the raven) and the bird's harmful betrayal of the infidelity of the god's "wife": the wife of Bath retells the tale of Midas's ass ears, which he confessed only to his wife (not to his barber, as in Ovid), who unwittingly spread the scandal by whispering it into the earth.

Educated Englishmen such as Spencer and Sidney would have read Ovid in the original, but translations began to appear for the wider reading public in Shakespeare's youth. Oddly, the first translation was only of the Narcissus episode (by T[homas] H[owell] in 1560) and the second was "The pleasant fable of Hermaphroditus and Salmacis" (Peend Thomas, 1565); both were beset with masses of introductory and paratextual material. Real accessibility came with Arthur Golding's translation of Ovid's first four books into English fourteen-syllable lines (1565), followed by his version of the whole poem in 1567. He too felt obliged to defend the *Metamorphoses* against accusations of immorality in his preface and accompanied his version with an explanatory verse epistle. Raphael Lyne has noted that Golding's translation represents a major break from the moralizing tradition simply "because it is what we would call a translation of Ovid . . . recognizing the right of the text to a life of its own is itself a change" (Lyne 2001: 53). It was Golding's version that opened up Ovid's poem to Shakespeare, who embraced the romance of Ovid's tales from his earliest plays.

The early *Titus Andronicus* is the most explicit in its characters' open citation of Latin authors (Seneca as well as Ovid) and goes beyond incidental references to Hecuba and Daedalus to use the grim tale of Tereus and Philomela as key to the barbarous rape by Tamora's sons. Jonathan Bate (1995: 79–88) calls it "the pivotal play in Shakespeare's early career." He notes that Shakespeare turned to poetry when the theaters were closed because of plague and found Golding's Ovid as source for his poem *Venus and Adonis*. At about the same time, rival players had actually included a dramatization of Philomela and Tereus in a work called *Four Plays in One*. Bate argues that *Titus* was both a sourceless play (as regards its main intrigue) and "composed out of a series of precedents in the dramatic repertoire and a series of patterns in Shakespeare's reading of the classics" (1995: 90). Thus, when Titus's brother Marcus finds his niece Lavinia mutilated (both tongue and hands were cut off), he interprets her state as that of Philomela:

> But sure, some Tereus hath deflowered thee,
> and lest thou shouldst detect him, cut thy tongue . . .
>
> . . . .
>
> fair Philomel, why she but lost her tongue,
> and in a tedious sampler sewed her mind,
> but, lovely niece, that means is cut from thee.

A craftier Tereus, cousin, hast thou met,
and he hath cut those pretty fingers off
that could have better sewed than Philomel. (2.3.25–6, 37–44)

It is perhaps more remarkable that Lavinia searches mutely for Ovid's poem (4.1.42) and points to "the tragic tale of Philomel" until her uncle shows her how to write in the sand guiding a stick with her teeth and feet. This too is almost certainly inspired by the *Metamorphoses:* the raped Io only inscribes her name (blessedly short) in the sand, but Lavinia somehow spells out the crime and the criminals: *"stuprum:* Chiron, Demetrius" (4.1.79). Thus, the Ovidian text both shapes the offense and guides its detection. Ironically, Titus's retaliation by cooking and serving the rapists to their mother comes far closer to the spirit of revenge in which Seneca's Atreus fed Thyestes his own children than to the Ovidian tragedy; but then Seneca himself had deliberately echoed Ovid's tale in his *Thyestes* and has his villain gloat over preparing an act of vengeance even worse than "the Thracian evil deed." Philomela would again be the significant reading of Imogen before she escapes rape in *Cymbeline.*

On a happier note, audiences who have never tasted Ovid still feel hilarious delight in the glorious absurdity of the "most lamentable comedy and most cruel death of Pyramus and Thisby" as rehearsed and performed by the mechanicals of *Midsummer Night's Dream.* But the *Dream* also offers more indirect homage, providing parallels to the divine deceptions of Mercury in Puck's mischief, first in metamorphosing Bottom into an ass, then in making Titania dote upon him. The strange confusions of the four mismatched lovers straying through the woods, enhanced by Puck's misapplication of his love charm to the wrong lovers, follow the same pattern as the punishment of Narcissus with self-love or the various bungled affairs of Apollo. Above all, a dreamlike atmosphere of discontinuity and inconsequentiality pervades the action of lords and citizens, craftsmen and fairy folk, that echoes on a more harmless, comic scale the pursuits and flights of *Metamorphoses* 1–5.

The Winter's Tale is an awkward comedy, opening with the prolonged episode of Leontes' unwarranted jealousy and the apparent death of his queen, Hermione. Where Shakespeare has learned most from Ovid (and diverges furthest from his Italian model, *Pandosto*) is in the "denouement" (after sixteen years) brought on when Paulina invites Leontes to admire her "Statue" of his dead queen:

> O thus she stood,
> even with such life of majesty, warm life,
> as now it coldly stands, when first I wooed her.
> I am ashamed. Doth not the stone rebuke me,
> for being more stone that it is? (5.3.34–7)

Paulina takes Venus's role, controlling the gradual revelation, until Leontes cries out to his friend Polixenes (63–8): "See, my Lord / would you not deem it breathed? And that those veins did verily bear blood? :: Masterly done; / the very life seems warm upon her lip. / :: The fixture of her eyes has motion in't, as we are mocked with art." Finally, Paulina commands a miracle: her living "statue" is to move and approach her husband, and he feels her living warmth, not daring to believe his senses, as they at last embrace. Thus, Shakespeare combines the illusion of an Ovidian transformation with the blessed reunion of an Aristotelian recognition scene.

In the introduction to his *Tales from Ovid,* Ted Hughes speaks of Shakespeare "lifting images or even whole passages nearly verbatim" (this surely goes too far) but finds "a more crucial connection . . . in their common taste for a tortured subjectivity and catastrophic extremes of passion that border on the grotesque" (1997: viii). This is perhaps what our own age seeks and so finds in all three poets, and the popularity of different episodes has varied with the tastes of a given time and place: not only their importance but the form given to them. Take Midas, whose ass's ears were celebrated by Chaucer and found their way onto Bottom's head. In the nineteenth century Nathaniel Hawthorne made Midas the theme of "The Golden Touch," one of two tales from the *Metamorphoses* included in his *Wonder Book* of moral tales for children. He specifically discards the ass's ears but gives Midas a little daughter, Mary*gold,* "whom nobody but myself ever heard of," and makes it the climax of Midas's folly when she runs to comfort her father and is turned into lifeless gold. Her father's grief is resolved only when he finds out from the god how to reverse the effect of his touch and restore her to life. And this was the version chosen for staging the New York production of *Metamorphoses,* which made its closure Midas's return with the healing water to revive his daughter. In her version for the Anglo-American Hoffman and Lasdun collection *After Ovid: The New Metamorphoses,* the feminist poet Carol Ann Duffy reverts to the domesticity of Chaucer's tale and composes a sort of elegy for Midas's wife. She is forced first to lock her bedroom door, then drive him away from their home; as the starving Midas suffers delusions and thinks he hears the music of Pan, her final thoughts lament the loss of "his warm hands on my skin, his touch" (pp. 12–13). I first read Hawthorne's other choice, "The Miraculous Pitcher," as a child, and loved the tale, which stays true to Ovid's narrative of Baucis and Philemon but turns the poor Mediterranean peasants into teetotal New England smallholders serving the gods butter and cheese from their cow. At the bidding of "Quicksilver's" magic serpent staff, the miraculous pitcher replenishes itself with milk, and the feast is a nursery tea of brown bread and honey. But the warmth of the old couple survives even Hawthorne's Victorian moralizing.

The tale of Arachne appeals to poets as an allegory of poetic creation. John Hollander, the poet and critic of poetry, re-created Ovid's tale in twentieth-century fashion by giving a voice to the victim. "Arachne's Story" in *Figurehead and Other Poems* follows Ovid closely but adds comment reflecting the values of a committed craftswoman:

> Weaving, admittedly can be the best
> Of work; onto the warp of unsignifying strength
> Are woven the threads of imaging that
> Do their unseen work of structure too,
> But can depict even while they draw
> The warp together: my images are thus
> Truly in and of the fabric, texture itself becoming
> Text, rather than lying like painting
> Lightly upon some canvas or some wall.

It was not to challenge her,
Like some idiot warrior going up against some
Other idiot warrior; say rather
That it was to hear the simultaneous song
Of two harmonious shuttles, nosing in
And out of their warp like dolphins out
Of their one blue and into another. (pp. 12–13)

The fate of Arachne is naturally one of Ted Hughes's selections from the *Metamorphoses*. He has enriched the memorable imagery of Ovid's narrative with more of his own. Thus, "The nymphs came down from the vines on Tmolus, / as butterflies to a garden, to flock stunned / around what flowered out of the warp and the weft under her fingers," outdoes *Metamorphoses* 6.15, and Hughes converts Arachne's angry stare at Minerva (6.34) into "she reared like a cobra scowling." In general, however, his version is as true to Ovid as it is fluent, only extending the final metamorphosis to represent Arachne in terms of her old skill:

she hangs from the thread that she spins
out of her belly.
Or ceaselessly weaves it into patterned webs
on a loom of leaves and grasses.
Her touches
deft and swift and light as when they were human. (*Tales
from Ovid*, p. 170)

(*Met.* 6.144–5: *cetera venter habet, de quo tamen illa remittit / stamen, et antiquas exercet aranea telas* [A stomach occupies the rest, from which she still emits a thread, and keeps her old loom busy]).

Part of Hughes's fame came to him as a poet of nature and the cruelty of wildlife: thus, it is natural that he should have chosen to translate the grim double horror of rape and mutilation, infanticide and cannibalism, that is, the story of Tereus, Philomela, and Procne. Similarly, Hollander was fascinated chiefly by the strange fusion of music and vocal melody from pain, and his *Philomel* is a complex and beautiful experiment across poetry and music: both the song-poem and the poet's own discussion add a new dimension to our understanding of Ovid. When the twelve-tone composer Milton Babbitt asked him to compose a poem for Bethany Beardsley to sing against an electronic musical text, including a tape of her own recorded voice, Hollander, perhaps recalling Philomela's threat to "fill the forest and stir the rocks as witnesses" (6.547), created a miniature dramatic scene comparable to Schoenberg's *Erwartung*. It has three movements. The first, "representing the Thracian woods initiating and then commenting in a choral way upon her singing," plays on the sounds of her name and that of Tereus, beginning with a scream that becomes the word "Feel!"

I feel	
I feel a million trees	
and the heat of trees.	TAPE: not true trees
I feel a million tears:	TAPE: not true tears—
is it Tereus I feel?	not true trees—
Is it Tereus I feel?	
	TAPE: not Tereus, not a true
	Tereus—
Feel a million filaments,	
fear the tearing, the feeling	
Trees, that are full of felony—	
Trees tear,	
and I hear,	
Families of tears—	

The second movement is "Philomel's dialogue with the birds around her, seeking their help in realizing her new identity as a bird," and Hollander describes the third as "that of song expounding itself." Philomel's song combines past and present in a sequence that alternates sets of four long lines to evoke past suffering with six short lines moving from the word "change" to her present bird existence:

Love's most hidden tongue throbbed in the barbarous
    daylight;
Then all became pain in one great scream of silence, fading,

Finally, as all the voices of feeling died in the west
And pain alone remained with remembering in my breast

I screamed in change,
Now all I can do
Is bewail that chase.
For now I range (refrain)
Thrashing, through
The woods of Thrace.

This work, the only modern music I know inspired by an episode from the *Metamorphoses,* has been recorded and should be heard
to convey its full and eerie power. But even without music, Ovid's
text was powerful enough to inspire Seneca, Chaucer, and Shakespeare, and Hughes responds fiercely to its challenge, again adding
his own imagery. Compare *Metamorphoses* 6.451–7 with

Once the two had met, there, mid-sentence,
Philomela herself—arrayed
In the wealth of a kingdom—entered:
Still unaware that her own beauty
Was the most astounding of her jewels.

She looked like one of those elfin queens
You hear about
Flitting through the depths of forests.
Tereus felt his blood alter thickly;
Suddenly he himself was like a forest,
When a drought wind explodes it into a firestorm. (*Tales
from Ovid,* p. 215)

Although the notion of elfin queens seems out of place, the simile succeeds in linking Philomela's forest world to Hughes's own
modified comparison of Tereus's lust to a forest fire. The thickening blood is Hughes, not Ovid, but powerful, as are his versions of
Ovid's similes (6.527–9) comparing Philomela to the victim of a
wolf or hawk: "Afterwards, she crouched in a heap, shuddering—
/ like a lamb, still clinging to life / after the wolf has savaged it /

And for some reason dropped it. Or like a dove, a bloody rag, still alive / Under the talons that stand on it." Unfortunately, his rendering of her reproaches with its short shrill lines falls short of Ovid's tragic decorum. But Hughes conveys brilliantly Procne's reaction to her sister's tapestry:

The tyrant's wife
Unrolled the tapestry and saw
The only interpretation
Was the ruin of her life.
She sat there, silent and unmoving,
As if she thought of something else entirely.

In these moments, her restraint
Was superhuman. But grief so sudden, so huge,
made mere words seem paltry. None could lift to her lips
One drop of its bitterness.
And tears were pushed aside

By the devouring single idea
Of revenge. Revenge
Had swallowed her whole being. She had plunged
Into a labyrinth of plotting
Where good and evil, right and wrong,
Forgot their differences.

Hughes does not falter throughout the climactic sequence that follows. He has proudly set this terrible narrative, which answers some barbarian streak in our present society, second to last in the sequence of twenty-four tales. And while readers may wish that Hughes had adapted other episodes (Medea, Ceyx and Alcyone, Baucis and Philemon) or regret that the poet's death prevented him from providing a complete version of the *Metamorphoses,* there is no evidence that he would have wished to fill in what he had passed over. Still, his choices deserve some comment. Golding first published only books 1–4, and these books provide ten of Hughes's choices. We have seen that Hughes includes Arachne and Tereus from book 6; he also "translates" Niobe but passes over Orpheus's own katabasis and death scene in books 10–11, in favor of Myrrha, Pygmalion, and Venus and Adonis, with Venus's cautionary tale of Atalanta and Meleager. In an age more sympathetic to warrior epic, Dryden translated large sections of books 1, 8, and 11–13, but apart from Orpheus's song recital, Hughes goes beyond book 8 only for the birth and death of Hercules, Peleus's wooing of Thetis, Midas, and the death of Cygnus. Without any Roman material, not to mention the final invocation of divine protection for Augustus, there could be no organic closure: the stage *Metamorphoses* faced the same challenge and ended with the loving and simultaneous death of Baucis and Philemon; the Hughes collection has substituted Pyramus and Thisbe. In the most recent discussion of both the composite Hoffman and Lasdun collection and Hughes's "two dozen renewals," John Henderson (1999) regrets the triteness of ending with this *Liebestod*. It would certainly have surprised Ovid.

Ovid had ended by proudly affirming the immortality of his poem, yet in a letter from exile (*Tristia* 1.7), he claims he tried to burn the *Metamorphoses*, seeing it as unfinished and perhaps as the *carmen* that had offended Augustus. He even compares his act to infanticide, and himself to Althaea, whose destruction of the log that stood for her son's life he had vividly portrayed in *Metamorphoses* 8.451–525. Yet Ovid somehow made sure that his poetic history of divine and human folly from chaos to "my times" did survive for generations to read and for writers and artists to perpetuate through their own visions. As its readers have changed, so has their reception of the poem, and for many critics it is this capacity for growth and change that constitutes the lasting vitality of the *Metamorphoses*.

Further Reading

Charles Martindale, *Ovid Renewed: Ovidian Influences on Literature and Art from the Middle Ages to the Twentieth Century* (Cambridge, 1988) (see especially Helen Cooper, "Chaucer and Ovid: A Question of Authority," 71–81, and Nigel Llewellyn, "Illustrating Ovid," 157–66); C. Martindale and M. Martindale, *Shakespeare and the Uses of*

Antiquity: An Introductory Essay (London, 1990); Leonard Barkan, *The Gods Made Flesh: Metamorphosis and the Pursuit of Paganism* (New Haven, 1990); Marina Warner, *Fantastic Metamorphoses, Other Worlds: Ways of Telling the Self* (Oxford, 2002); S. A. Brown, *The "Metamorphosis" of Ovid: From Chaucer to Ted Hughes* (New York, 1999); Shakespeare, *Titus Andronicus,* Arden Shakespeare, series 3, ed. J. Bate (London, 1995); *The Winter's Tale*, Arden Shakespeare, ed. J. H. Pafford (London, 1903; repr. 1991); R. Lyne, *Ovid's Changing Worlds: English Metamorphoses, 1567–1632* (Oxford, 2001); and R. Lyne, "Ovid in English Translation," in *The Cambridge Companion to Ovid,* ed. P. R. Hardie (Cambridge, 2002), 249–63.

The *Cambridge Companion to Ovid* includes a new study, "Ovid and Art," by Christopher Allen, whose illustrations for Titian, Bernini, and Poussin are cited in this chapter. Other Titian references are given from Martindale 1988 and the catalogue of the Venice exhibition *Titian: Prince of Painters* (Venice, 1990). The Poussin illustrations and the comment on Poussin's use of *Metamorphoses* are taken from Anthony Blunt's *Nicolas Poussin: The Mellon Lectures* (Washington, D.C., 1967).

Nathaniel Hawthorne's two tales come from *A Wonder Book* (1851), reprinted in vol. 7 of the centenary edition published by Ohio State University Press, Columbus. The poems of John Hollander are cited from "A Poem for Music: Remarks on the Composition of *Philomel,*" in *Vision and Resonance: Two Senses of Poetic Form* (New York, 1975), 289–306, and *Figurehead and Other Poems* (New York, 1999). Carol Ann Duffy's "Mrs. Midas" is taken from *After Ovid: The New Metamorphoses,* ed. M. Hoffman and J. Lasdun (London, 1994). The versions of Ted Hughes are from *Tales from Ovid: Twenty-four Passages from the "Metamorphoses"* (London, 1997). For John Henderson's critique of *After Ovid* and *Tales from Ovid*, see Philip R. Hardie, Alessandro Barchiesi, and Stephen Hinds, eds., *Ovidian Transformations: Essays on Ovid's "Metamorphoses" and Its Reception* (Cambridge, 1999), 301-16.

APPENDIX I

Ovid's Poetical Works

1 | Love Elegy (23 B.C.E.?–2 C.E.)

Ovid's earliest love elegies pretend to be autobiographical, first-person experience. The three books of *Amores* (Love affairs) were originally published as five books, according to the prefatory epigram, but Ovid does not
make it clear whether he reduced five books to three by discarding some
elegies, by regrouping them, or by both subtracting some poems and introducing new ones. Individual poems would have been composed before
any publication in book form. During the same period Ovid wrote the
Heroides (Letters from heroines) 1–15, a collection of love letters of ancient
heroines "in character," resembling dramatic monologues. These were followed by *Heroides* 16–21, three pairs of love letters between Paris and
Helen, Leander and Hero, and Acontius and Cydippe. Toward the end of this
time books 1 and 2 of *Ars amatoria* (Art of love), ostensibly manuals of seduction for young men, began to circulate. *Ars amatoria* 3, instructing young
women, and *Remedia amoris* (Cures for love) followed soon after, probably
in response to the success of the earlier books.

It is harder to work out when these books were written. The *Amores*
react to Horace's *Odes* 1–3 (23 B.C.E.) and Propertius's third book (published about the same time). The latest internal historical allusion is to the
defeat of the Sygambri in 8 B.C.E. (Am. 1.14. 45–50). *Amores* 2.18, probably
written for the second edition (published by 2 B.C.E.?), reports that Ovid

had begun a tragedy but implies (like *Amores* 3.1) that he was distracted from it and was now composing "arts of love," usually understood as the *Ars amatoria* (2.18.13 and 19–20). It also names many of the letters of heroines (2.18.20–5). The first book of *Ars amatoria* refers to Gaius Caesar's expedition of 1 B.C.E., and it is generally thought that all three books were published, with the *Remedia,* by 2 C.E. There is also an unfinished poem on cosmetics (*Medicamina faciei femineae*), which may be from this early period.

2 | Tragedy: *Medea* (before 2 B.C.E.?)

In *Amores* 3.1 Ovid describes an imaginary meeting with the Muses of Tragedy and Elegy, in which Tragedy demands his services, but Elegy detains him. His now lost tragedy *Medea,* almost certainly treating Medea's infanticide at Corinth, must have been written toward the end of his main output of love elegy, but there is no other evidence to date it. It was probably composed with dialogue in regular iambic trimeters and with choral interludes in anapaestic and other lyric meters.

3 | Hexameter Epic: *Metamorphoses* (2 B.C.E.?–17 C.E.)

Ovid seems to have begun the fifteen books of the *Metamorphoses,* his only hexameter poem, even before he completed the books of *Ars amatoria.* In *Tristia* 2 Ovid tells Augustus that he has composed a poem recording world history from chaos to "your times." He also represents the *Metamorphoses* as unfinished, but unlike *Fasti* (see section 4 below) the poem reached its intended conclusion with the future deification of Augustus and is only unfinished in the sense that he hoped to make further refinements. While Ovid may have begun *Metamorphoses* before *Fasti,* or simply composed the narrative poem more rapidly than the etiological calendar poem, echoes and cross-references between the two large "historical" poems make it clear that he was composing both during the same years.

4 | Calendar Poem (1 C.E.?–17 C.E.)

In *Tristia* 2 Ovid claims that he has already written *Fasti* (Calendar days), twice six books honoring Augustus by describing the festivals and legends associated with the twelve months of the Roman calendar, but that exile interrupted his composition. Only six books survive, covering January through June. There are clear indications that he returned to the poem after Augustus's death in 14 but, instead of continuing into the second half of the year, began to remodel what he had written, starting with a dedication, not to Tiberius, the new princeps, but to the crown prince Germanicus. The poem was left unfinished when Ovid died in 17 C.E.

5 | Elegies from Exile (8–17 C.E.)

Immediately after being relegated to Tomis, Ovid began the first book of his *Tristia* (Poems of sadness), of which several describe his troubled journey. *Tristia* 2 consists of one long poem: a plea to the emperor defending the innocence of his *Art of Love* and begging for a kinder place of exile. After three more books, in the form of letters to his wife and unidentified friends and patrons, Ovid began a new series, *Epistulae ex Ponto* (Letters from the Black Sea), in about 12 C.E. First was a set of three books addressed to named friends and published together; these are actively concerned with the surrounding people and landscape. The fourth book, composed after the death of Augustus, was apparently published after Ovid's own death in 17 C.E. and may not have been arranged by the poet. A long and strange curse-poem, *Ibis* (The dirty bird), written in imitation of a lost work of Callimachus, was perhaps composed between the *Tristia* and *Epistulae ex Ponto*. The unfinished catalogue of fish and seafood called *Halieutica* may also be an Ovidian poem from exile.

APPENDIX 2

Outline of the *Metamorphoses*

The simplified synopsis of the *Metamorphoses* on the following pages is designed to help readers find the major stories and see how they fit into their immediate context. The main figures and themes that sustain the narrative are indicated in capital letters, and in each narrative or subordinate tale, actual metamorphoses are indicated in italics.

BOOK 1.1–4 PROEM. 1.5–162 COSMOGONY AND CREATION OF LIFE. 1–75 From chaos to an ordered world, populated with stars and animal life. 76–88 Mankind created to control animals and respect the gods. 89–150 The ages of man: golden age (89–112); silver, born with reign of Jupiter (113–24); bronze; iron age of greed and impiety (125–50). 151–62 The giants' failed assault on Olympus and earth's new human creation from their blood.

1.163–261 JUPITER CALLS COUNCIL OF THE GODS; PROPOSES TO DESTROY MANKIND BECAUSE OF IMPIETY OF LYCAON. 165–239 Jupiter's evidence: Lycaon punished by *transformation into a wolf*. 240–61 Jupiter's decision to drown humanity in universal flood.

1.262–437 FLOOD AND NEW CREATION. 262–312 Jupiter's winds and rains and Neptune's rivers flood the earth, sweeping humans and animals away. 313–437 The flood recedes when only Deucalion and Pyrrha are left. Advised by oracle of Themis, they *create a new race of man by throwing stones behind them. Natural heat and moisture re-create animal life.*

1.438–567 APOLLO AND DAPHNE. 438–51 Apollo slays Python and provokes his brother Cupid into wounding him with love for the nymph Daphne, herself immunized by a lead-tipped arrow. 452–567 Unable to escape his wooing, Daphne begs earth to save her and is *transformed into a laurel tree,* which Apollo embraces and promises to honor.

1.568–750 THE TRANSFORMATION AND RESCUE OF IO. 568–667 Jupiter rapes Io *and turns her into a cow* to hide her from Juno, who sets Argos to guard her. When Io makes herself known to her father, Argos puts her to flight. 668–723 Jupiter sends Mercury to save her by lulling Argos to sleep with *the metamorphosis of Syrinx by Pan.* 724–50 Jupiter begs Juno's pardon and *Io resumes human shape and speech* by the Nile, to be worshiped as a goddess, along with her child, Epaphus.

1.750–1–BOOK 2.400 PHAETHON. 1.751–2.1–48 Phaethon sets out to find his father. Description of the Sun's palace doors, retinue, and chariot. Phaethon exploits Sun's promise and demands to drive the chariot. 49–149 His father's instructions. 150–213 Phaethon loses control, horses run amok scorching Earth. 214–318 Jupiter answers Earth's appeal by striking Phaethon dead with his thunderbolt. 319–80 Mourning of his mother and *sisters, turned into poplars; his lover Cycnus becomes a swan.* 381–400 The Sun grudgingly resumes his daily journey.

2.401–530 CALLISTO is raped by Jupiter, disguised as Diana. She bears a son, then *is turned into a bear.* To prevent the son, Arcas, from shooting his own mother, Jupiter transforms both into stars. 531–41 *Argos's eyes set in tail of Juno's peacock.*

2.542–632 The raven's betrayal of Coronis, killed by jealous Apollo. 633–75 Ocyroe prevented from foretelling rebirth of Aesclepius *by being turned into a horse.* 676–707 Mercury steals Apollo's cattle, *punishes informer* BATTUS *by turning him into a stone.* 708–832 Mercury woos Herse: *he eliminates jealous Aglauros by turning her into a stone.* 2.833–Book 3.1–5 Jupiter disguises himself as a bull to carry Europa over the sea from Phoenicia to Boeotia, and her brother Cadmus is sent to find her or remain an exile.

3.5–315 CADMUS'S THEBAN DYNASTY. 3.5–137 Cadmus kills dragon, founds Thebes with men *sprung from dragon's teeth*. 138–252 Diana is surprised by Actaeon while bathing and *changes him into a stag*, which is killed by his own dogs. 253–315 Semele, courted by Jupiter, is tricked by Juno into asking him to appear in full form, dies consumed by his fire. Her son, Bacchus, born from Jupiter's thigh, is reared by Ino.

3.316–38 TEIRESIAS, made arbiter between Jupiter and Juno, *after seven years as a woman*, is blinded by Juno.

339–510 ECHO AND NARCISSUS. Echo is punished by Juno, only able to repeat others' speech. Because of her vain love of Narcissus, *she wastes away to a mere voice* when he dies pining for his own image in a forest pool.

3.511–733 PENTHEUS. 511–76 Pentheus orders seizure of followers of Bacchus. 577–691 Acoetes's tale: Bacchus punishes pirates *by turning them into dolphins*. 692–700 Imprisoned by Pentheus, Acoetes is miraculously released. 701–33 Spying Pentheus is captured by bacchantes and torn apart by mother and aunts, who see him as a lion.

BOOK 4.1–415 THE MINYEIDES. 1–54 Refusing to worship, the daughters of Minyas stay at home weaving and telling stories. (1) 55–166 PYRAMUS AND THISBE each commits suicide, believing the other dead; *fruit of mulberry tree turns black*. (2) 167–270 THE SUN, LEUCOTHOE, and CLYTIE. 167–89 Sun betrays adultery of Mars and Venus. 190–270 Sun rapes Leucothoe, disguised as her mother. Jealous Clytie *turned into sunflower*. (3) 271–388 SALMACIS RAPES AND EMASCULATES HERMAPHRODITUS when he resists seduction in her pool. 389–415 *Bacchus turns Minyeides into bats*.

4.416–562 JUNO PUNISHES INO AND ATHAMAS. 4.416–542 Juno descends to Hades, sending Tisiphone to madden Athamas and Ino. Neptune *saves Ino and Palaemon by making them sea deities*. 543–62 *Ino's maids transformed into seabirds*.

4.563–603 CADMUS AND HARMONIA *transformed into pair of serpents*.

4.604–BOOK 5.249 PERSEUS. 604–62 *Perseus uses head of slain Medusa to petrify Atlas*. 663–739 Rescues Andromeda, killing sea monster. 740–52

Medusa petrifies seaweed, creating coral. 753–89 Marriage to Andromeda. 790–804 *Tale of Medusa's transformation.* 5.1–249 Phineus and retinue break into wedding feast. Perseus uncovers the head of Medusa to *petrify his enemies, turning Phineus and others into statues.*

5.250–678 THE MUSES' CONTEST. 250–340 *Creation of Hippocrene by Pegasus's hoof.* Muses attacked by Pyreneus; challenge of Pierides and song insulting Olympians. 341–678 CERES' QUEST FOR PERSEPHONE told by Calliope. 341–450 Dis abducts Persephone, *transforms Cyane into spring.* 451–61 Searching Ceres *turns rude boy into lizard.* 462–571 Obtains agreement from Jupiter for Persephone to spend half of the year aboveground (533–63 *Informer Ascalaphus turned into owl; attendants become Sirens*). 572–641 Arethusa's tale; Diana saves her from Alpheus *by turning her into freshwater spring.* 642–78 Triptolemus brings agriculture to Athens. *Pierides turned into magpies.*

BOOK 6.1–145 MINERVA AND ARACHNE. Goddess and girl compete; Arachne's skilled tapestry denounces divine lust. Jealous Minerva *turns her into a spider.*

6.146–312 APOLLO AND DIANA SLAY CHILDREN OF NIOBE, who has mocked their mother, Latona. *Grieving Niobe becomes a weeping cliff.* 313–381 Latona's earlier vengeance on Lycian peasants *turned into frogs.* 382–400 Apollo flays Marsyas for competing against him in a musical contest. *Marsyas becomes a river.* 401–23 Only Athens does not share Pelops's mourning for Niobe.

6.424–674 TEREUS, PROCNE, AND PHILOMELA. 424–50 Pandion marries daughter Procne to Thracian ally Tereus. 451–560 Escorting Philomela from Athens, Tereus rapes and mutilates her. 561–665 She weaves message to Procne, who brings her home; together they celebrate Bacchanalia, kill son Itys, and feed his flesh to Tereus. 666–74 *They are transformed into hoopoe, swallow, and nightingale.*

6.675–721 Pandion refuses Orithyia to BOREAS; raped, she bears Boreas Zetes and Calais, who *sprout wings at puberty* and sail on the Argo.

BOOK 7.1–452 MEDEA. 1–158 Falls in love with Jason; saves him from bulls and *earthborn dragon warriors* and snatches fleece from dragon; they reach Iolcos. 159–296 Using magic herbs, *Medea rejuvenates Aeson.* 297–349 Deceives Pelias's daughters into slaughtering their father. 350–403 Escapes to Corinth (391–7), then Athens.

7.404–52 THESEUS comes to Athens, escapes Medea's poison; recognized by Aegeus and honored with hymn.

7.453–666 AEACUS AND THE MYRMIDONS. 453–522 Athens sends Cephalus to seek help against Minos from Aegina. 523–666 Aeacus tells how, after plague of Aegina, Jupiter helped him by *sending an army of ants that became the soldiers he needed to fight Minos.*

7.667–862 CEPHALUS AND PROCRIS. Asked about dog and javelin, Cephalus tells of his marriage ruined by jealous misunderstandings. (753–93 The magic dog chases fox, *both transformed into stone.*) 794–862 Procris spies on Cephalus hunting; he wounds her by mistake but proves his fidelity before she dies.

7.863–BOOK 8.1–5 Cephalus's safe return with the ant soldiers from Megara.

8.6–151 SCYLLA AND MINOS. Scylla of Megara falls in love, takes father Nisus's head to enemy king Minos, asking to be his bride. When he sails away, she leaps into the sea after him and *is turned into a seabird, the shearwater.*

8.152–235 DAEDALUS AND ICARUS. Daedalus creates labyrinth for Minotaur. Theseus slays Minotaur, abandons Ariadne, *whose crown Bacchus sets in heaven.* Daedalus makes wings to fly away, but Icarus flies too high, melting wings, and drowns.

8.236–59 Daedalus's jealous murder of Perdix, *turned by Minerva into a partridge.*

8.260–444 THE CALYDONIAN BOAR HUNT. Theseus and others hunt the wild boar, wounded by Atalanta; Meleager rewards his beloved Atalanta, kills mother Althaea's brothers in quarrel over prize. 445–532 Althaea, enraged, destroys brand that maintains her son's life, and Meleager dies as it burns. 533–46 *Mourning sisters turned into birds.*

8.547–610 THESEUS ENTERTAINED BY ACHELOUS. Achelous's rape of nymph Perimele, *whom he saves from her angry father by turning her into an island.*

8.611–724 PEIRITHOUS DISPUTES DIVINE POWER TO IMPOSE TRANSFOR-
MATION. Lelex refutes him with tale of BAUCIS AND PHILEMON, who welcome gods unaware and are saved from separation in death by *transformation into trees*.

8.725–889 ACHELOUS AFFIRMS SELF-TRANSFORMING POWERS OF SHAPE-
SHIFTERS. ERYSICHTHON AND MNESTRA. Punished by Ceres with unquench-
able hunger for destroying her sacred tree, Erysichthon sells his daughter
Mnestra, who is enabled to escape by *Neptune's gift of shape-shifting*. Death
of Erysichthon by self-consumption.

BOOK 9.1–403 HERCULES. 1–97 Shape-shifting Achelous defeated by Hercules, who gives broken horn to nymphs as cornucopia. 98–272 DEIANEIRA
AND NESSUS. Defeated Nessus gives Deianeira poisoned cloth, which she
unwittingly sends to Hercules as love token. Consumed by its fire Hercules
ascends pyre on Oeta and *is made a god*.

9.273–323 MOTHERS' TALES: ALCMENE AND IOLE. How Galanthis tricked
Juno, *who turned her into a weasel*. 324–93 How Dryope *was turned into a tree*
for plucking lotus. 394–449 *Rejuvenation of Iolaus*: Themis refuses to extend
the privilege to him.

9.450–665 BYBLIS AND CAUNUS. Byblis's incestuous passion for her twin
brother. When he goes into exile to escape her, she pursues him until *she
becomes a stream*.

9.666–797 IPHIS. Reared in disguise as a boy, the girl Iphis falls in love with
Ianthe. Isis answers her mother's prayer and *changes her into a young man* before the wedding.

BOOK 10.1–85 ORPHEUS AND EURYDICE. Orpheus goes to Hades to beg
return of dead Eurydice but loses her by looking back; rejects love of
women. 86–142 As he sings to lyre, trees gather, including the cypress
(106–42 Cyparissus *transformed by Apollo*).

10.143–739 SONGS OF ORPHEUS about boys beloved by gods and illicit loves.
143–61 Ganymede. 162–219 Accidental death of Hyacinthus, *turned into
the flower by grieving Apollo*, who institutes festival of Hyacinthia. 220–42

Inhospitable Cerastae *afflicted with horns;* brazen and promiscuous Propoetides *turned to stone.*

10.243–97 PYGMALION loathes women: creates statue of maiden, prays to
love such a pure being, and with the help of Venus *brings it to life;* they have
a son, Paphos, grandfather of Myrrha.

10.298–514 MYRRHA. 298–475 Myrrha falls in love with her father and tricks
him into incest; he drives her away. 476–514 Escaping to wilderness, *she becomes a myrrh tree* and gives birth to Adonis.

10.515–739 ADONIS AND VENUS. 515–707 Loving Adonis, Venus warns him
against hunting dangerous prey like lions, explaining (560–707) the ingratitude of ATALANTA AND HIPPOMENES. Venus helped Hippomenes beat
Atalanta in the footrace but *turned them into lions* when they lustfully de-
filed her shrine with their intercourse. 708–39 Adonis ignores her warning and hunts the wild boar that fatally wounds him. She mourns him, in-
stituting Adonia, *and he is transformed into a scarlet anemone.*

BOOK 11.1–84 BACCHANTES lynch Orpheus. Angry Bacchus *turns them into
trees.*

11.85–193 MIDAS welcomes Bacchus to Phrygia: asks god for golden touch,
suffers, and purges himself, *leaving gold dust in Tmolus.* Midas misjudges contest of Apollo and Pan; *develops ass's ears.* Servant whispers his secret to the
earth but *grasses spread the tale.*

11.194–409 PELEUS. 194–217 Laomedon, helped by Apollo to build walls
of Troy, cheats; Hercules sacks Troy and gives Hesione to Telamon since
Peleus is married. 218–65 Peleus, advised by Proteus, captures shape-shifting
Thetis and fathers Achilles. 266–409 Goes to Ceyx to be purged of blood
guilt for Phocus. 291–345 Daedalion (angered by rape of daughter Chione)
turned into hawk. 346–409 Peleus's flocks attacked; asks Ceyx for aid.

11.410–748 CEYX AND ALCYONE. 410–73 Ceyx travels to Clarus, despite
his loving wife's pleas. 474–572 Ceyx drowned in shipwreck. 573–673
Distressed by Alcyone's prayers, Juno asks Sleep to send shape-shifting
Morpheus to Alcyone as dead Ceyx. 674–748 Rushing to shore, Alcyone

finds drowned Ceyx and embraces him. *Transformed into halcyon birds, they nest each year on calm waters.*

11.749–95 Priam's son AESACUS, grieving for lost Hesperie, is *transformed by Thetis into diving bird.*

BOOK 12.1–66 TROJAN WAR: Rumor of Greeks sailing from Aulis reaches Troy. 67–167 First casualties. Combat of Achilles with impenetrable Cycnus; throttled *Cycnus is turned into a swan.* 168–209 Nestor's tale of Caenis, who was compensated for being raped *by Neptune with change to a male, Caeneus.* 210–392 BRAWL OF CENTAURS AT LAPITH WEDDING. 393–428 Cyllarus and Hylonome. 429–535 Heroism and death of Caeneus.

12.536–79 Tlepolemus recalls his father Hercules' defeat of centaurs. Nestor tells how Hercules killed Nestor's brother *Periclymenus the shape-shifter in form of eagle.* 580–619 Neptune and Apollo contrive death of Achilles.

12.620–BOOK 13.1–381 AJAX AND ULYSSES compete for arms of Achilles. 382–98 Defeated Ajax stabs himself; *from his blood springs a hyacinth flower inscribed with his name.*

13.399–421 Troy is seized and burned, and women captives are taken to ships. 422–564 In Thrace HECUBA witnesses sacrifice of Polyxena, finds murdered Polydorus, and avenges herself on Polymestor. 565–75 Thracians stone Hecuba, who *is transformed into a bitch.*

13.576–622 Aurora protests to Jupiter at lack of honor for son MEMNON. His soul *becomes a bird; his mourning sisters become flocks of fighting birds.*

13.623–14.608 AENEAS. 623–42 Aeneas escapes with Anchises and Ascanius to Thrace, then Delos. 643–705 Host Anius tells of lost daughters, rescued by Bacchus, who *turned them into doves.* Gives them shield depicting *miraculous birth* of twin warriors from sacrifice of maidens at Thebes. 706–34 They travel to Crete, then Buthrotum, then Straits of Messina; beset by Scylla and Charybdis.

13.735–14.75 SCYLLA AND GALATEA exchange stories. 750–897 Galatea loves Acis but is wooed by Cyclops, who crushes Acis in fury. Acis *trans-*

formed into a river. 898–915 Scylla shuns sea god Glaucus, who loves her. 916–65 His tale of *resurrected fish and his own change into a sea deity.* 13.965–14.39 Glaucus consults Circe, who offers herself and is rejected.

BOOK 14.40–74 Circe poisons Scylla's bathing pool, *and she becomes a monster girt with dogs, seizing Ulysses' sailors, then turned into rock* before she can harm Trojans.

75–100 AENEAS visits Dido's Carthage, Acestes' Sicily and Pithecoussa, *where Cercopes turned into monkeys.* 101–57 Consults Sibyl of Cumae, who tells how she has suffered and is fading away from Apollo's gift of immortality without youth.

14.158–434 ACHAEMENIDES AND MACAREUS. 158–222 Achaemenides tells of the Cyclops and his survival until rescued by Aeneas. 223–75 Macareus tells of Ulysses' visit to Aeolus, Laestrygones, and Circe. 276–307 *Comrades turned into pigs, then restored.* 308–434 Maid tells of LOVERS PICUS AND CANENS and Circe's cruel *transformation of Picus into a woodpecker;* Canens *wastes away entirely from grief.*

14.435–608 AENEAS IN LATIUM. 435–56 Aeneas comes to Latium and fights Turnus, with help from Evander. 457–512 Diomedes refuses help because his men have been *turned into birds.* 513–26 *Nymphs turn Apulian shepherd into wild olive.* 527–65 Turnus sets fire to Aeneas's ships, which are rescued by Cybele, *who transforms them into sea nymphs.* 566–80 Sack of Ardea, from which *heron rises to skies.* 581–608 Apotheosis of Aeneas.

14.609–851 Successive kings of Alba, with interlude (622–771) on love of shape-shifting Vertumnus for Pomona (695–765 Tale of Anaxarete, who was *turned into stone* for disdaining Iphis, who hanged himself for love). 772–851 ROMULUS and founding of Rome. 772–804 Naiads obstruct invading Sabines *with sulfurous springs.* 805–51 Death of Romulus, taken up to heaven as Quirinus; deification of his loyal wife, Hersilia.

BOOK 15.1–59 Numa goes to Croton, learns of *miraculous acquittal of Myscelus.*

15.60–478 Preaching of Pythagoras. 75–142 Denounces sacrifice and eating of animals. 143–236 Explains natural change. 237–417 Lists miraculous physical changes. 418–52 Teaches rise and fall of cities and rise of Rome as forecast by Helenus to Aeneas. 453–78 Repeats warning against harming animal souls by hunting or eating them.

15.479–546 Death of Numa. Egeria not consoled by Hippolytus-Virbius's tale of his death and *resurrection, is turned into a spring* by Diana. 547–565 *The spear of Romulus sprouts leaves.* 566–621 General Cipus *grows horns,* hides them with laurel, and tells Romans they must drive him away or even kill him to prevent him from becoming a king. Goes into voluntary exile outside city.

15.622–744 Special invocation to Muses introduces COMING OF AESCULAPIUS TO ROME. Envoys sent by senate bring serpent god by sea from Epidaurus to Antium and Ostia. There Vesta, protectress of Trojan fires, welcomes him into Rome, the world capital, and the foreign god settles on Tiber Island.

15.745–851 CAESAR. 745–806 Caesar is god in his own city, now that his victories *have turned him into a new star.* Yet his greatest achievement was to be father of Augustus. Venus foresaw the threat to his life, and the gods sent dreadful portents but could not avert fate. 807–42 Jupiter tells Venus that Caesar has completed his life's work and it is time for him to join the gods: this Venus will accomplish, aided by his son. After foretelling the future victories of OCTAVIAN (now in Ovid's past time), Jupiter prophesies other victories still to come, domestic reforms, and dynastic success. 843–51 Venus saves Caesar's soul, *which soars to heaven as a comet,* happy to be outdone by his son.

15.852–70 CAESAR AUGUSTUS is praised as Jupiter's regent on earth, and Ovid prays for his long life until he is ready to enter heaven.

15.871–9 The poet claims immortality for his own work, which will *carry him above the stars to be read wherever Rome rules on earth and through all ages.*

Index of Persons

Mythical and historical persons in *Metamorphoses* are in lowercase; ancient and modern writers and artists are in uppercase.

Allecto, Fury in Virgil, 48, 111
Alpheus, river, seeks to rape Arethusa,
    64
Althaea, mother of Meleager, causes
    his death in revenge for her
    brothers, 94, 150
Andromeda, Ethiopian princess
    rescued from sea-monster by
    Perseus, 91, 106
ANTONINUS LIBERALIS, Greek
    second-century C.E. collector of
    tales of metamorphosis, 14
Apollo, twin child with Diana of
    Jupiter and Latona
    flays Marsyas, 56
    performs in concert, 56
    pursues Daphne, 63
    slays children of Niobe, 69–70
    slays Python, 122
APOLLONIUS RHODIUS,
    third-century B.C.E. author
    of *Argonautica*, 6, 74, 120
APULEIUS, second-century C.E.
    author of *Metamorphoses* ("Golden
    Ass"), 133, 140
Arachne, skilled weaver punished
    by Minerva, 53–55, 145 (Hol-
    lander), 146 (Hughes)
ARATUS, third-century B.C.E.
    author of astronomical poem, 120
Arethusa (nymph), pursued by
    Alpheus, rescued by Diana, 64
Argos, many-eyed monster set to
    watch Io by Juno, 16–17
    his eyes in peacock's tail, 117
Ariadne, 6
    "Bacchus and Ariadne" (Titian), 135
Asclepius. *See* Aesculapius
Atalanta
    beloved of Meleager, 93
    runner and lover of Hippomenes, 81

Atlas, African king turned into moun-
    tain by Perseus, 90
Augustus, born Octavius, adopted as
    Gaius Iulius Caesar Octavianus,
    3, 28, 55, 98, 117, 122, 123
    deifies his father, Julius, himself in
    due course to become a god,
    102–3
Aurora, mother of Memnon,
    supplicates Jupiter, 72–73
Autonoe, daughter of Cadmus,
    mother of Actaeon, 38

Bacchus, child of Jupiter and Semele,
    38
    destroys Pentheus, 39–40
Battus, dishonest shepherd turned to
    stone by Mercury, 125–6
Baucis, wife of Philemon, rewarded
    for entertaining gods, 82, 87, 134,
    145 (Hawthorne)
BERNINI, Italian seventeenth-
    century sculptor, 139
BOIOS (BOIO), Greek author of col-
    lection of bird-metamorphoses,
    14
Boreas (north wind), lover of
    Orithyia, 106
BRUEGEL, PETER, sixteenth-
    century Flemish painter, 134
Byblis, incestuously in love with twin
    brother Caunus, 75

Cacus, monster killed by Hercules, 94
Cadmus, brother of Europa, married
    Harmonia, 14, 36–38, 87, 105
    father of Agave, Autonoe, Ino, and
    Semele (q.v.)
Caeneus/Caenis, transgendered
    warrior, 62–63, 110
Caesar (Julius), adoptive father of

Octavian, murdered, then deified,
15, 102–3, 117
CALLIMACHUS, third-century
B.C.E. Hellenistic poet and
scholar, ix, 6, 25, 120
  Aitia, 131
  Glaucus, 131
  Hecale, 120, 126–27
  Hymn to Apollo, 122
Calliope, Muse, her epic "Rape of
Persephone," 53
Callisto, daughter of Lycaon, raped by
Jupiter, mother of Arcas, 25, 63
CALVUS, first-century B.C.E. author
of *Io*, friend of Catullus, 6, 16,
120
Canens (nymph), loved by Picus, 11–12
Castor and Pollux (Dioscuri), 15, 93
CATULLUS, his "Marriage of Peleus
and Thetis," 6, 29, 120
Centaurs, brawl at wedding of
Peirithous, 63. *See also* Chiron,
Cyllarus, Hylonome
Cephalus, Athenian prince and
husband of Procris, 83–85
Ceres (Greek Demeter), mother of
Persephone, 53, 63–64
punishes Erysichthon, 111-12
Ceyx, husband of Alcyone, drowned
on voyage, 82, 85–87, 134, 141
Charybdis, sea-monster, 9
CHAUCER, *Book of the Duchess,
Legend of Good Women, House of
Fame, Canterbury Tales*, 141
Chione, raped by Apollo and Mercury,
64
Chiron, benevolent centaur, father of
Ocyroe, 108, 109, 126.
CINNA, first-century B.C.E author of
Zmyrna, friend of Catullus, 6, 79,
120

Cipus, Roman general who refused to
become king, 101–2
Circe, enchantress, bewitches Scylla,
Ulysses' men, Picus, 8–9, 10–12
CLAUDIAN, fourth-century C.E.
Latin poet, 140
Clymene, mother of Phaethon, 18, 34,
69
Cupid, wounds brother Apollo, 122
Cyane, Sicilian nymph, 64
Cyclops. *See* Polyphemus
Cycnus, kinsman and lover of
Phaethon, 34
warrior son of Neptune, 98–99, 113
Cyllarus, centaur, lover of Hylonome,
109
painted by Piero di Cosimo, 135
Cyparissus, boy beloved by Apollo, 77

Daedalion, brother of Ceyx, 85, 87
Daedalus, craftsman and father of
Icarus, 32, 58, 108, 140, 141
Danae, raped by Jupiter, mother of
Perseus, 12
painted by Titian, 135
DANTE, *Purgatorio*, 139–40
Daphne (nymph), daughter of Peneus,
pursued by Apollo, 63, 122. *See
also* Poussin, Bernini
Deianeira, wife of Hercules, pursued
by Nessus; causes Hercules'
death, 95
DEMOCRITUS, Greek fifth-century
natural philosopher, 22
Deucalion, son of Prometheus,
husband of Pyrrha, 29–30, 82
Diana, twin child of Jupiter and
Latona with Apollo, punishes
Actaeon, 38–39
  Diana and Actaeon (Titian), 138 fig. 3
  Diana and Callisto (Titian), 135

Dis, god of Underworld (also called
Hades), 53
DRYDEN, John, translated books of
Metamorphoses, 150
Dryope, sister of Iole, turned into
lotus tree, 68–69

Earth, goddess mother of giants, 27
protests at Phaethon's destructive
ride, 33
Echo, punished by Juno with loss of
independent speech; pines for
Narcissus, 44–46
Egeria (nymph), consort of Numa,
101
EMPEDOCLES, Sicilian Greek sixth-
century natural philosopher, 23
ENNIUS, second-century Italian epic
and tragic poet, 6, 75
imitated, 93, 100
Eratosthenes, third-century B.C.E.
geographer and poet, 23–24
Erysichthon, father of Mnestra,
punished by Ceres with insatiable
hunger, 111–12, 134
EURIPIDES, fifth-century Athenian
tragic poet
Bacchae, 14, 38
Hecuba, 71–72
Medea, 75
Phaethon, 32
Europa, sister of Cadmus, raped by
Jupiter, mother of Minos, 12,
36, 54
Rape of Europa (Titian), 135
Eurylochus, 8, 10–11

Fama. *See* Rumor
Furies. *See* Allecto, Tisiphone

Galanthis, loyal maid of Alcmene,
67–68

Galatea (nymph), lover of Acis, loved
in vain by Polyphemus, 128–29
GALLUS, poet, older contemporary
of Ovid, 14, 121
GIULIO ROMANO, Italian sixteenth-
century painter, 135
Glaucus, fisherman and lover of Scylla;
becomes sea-god, 10, 106
GOLDING, Arthur, first English
translator of *Metamorphoses*, 142

HAWTHORNE, Nathaniel, *A Wonder
Book*, 144
Hecuba, widow of Priam, king
of Troy, mother of Hector,
Polyxena, Polydorus, 71–72
Helen, wife of Menelaus, eloped with
Paris, 8, 55
Helenus, Trojan prince who settled in
Epirus; his prophecy to Aeneas,
117
Hercules (Gk. Heracles), son of
Jupiter and Alcmene, 15
his birth, 67
deification, 95–96
labors and travels, 94
Hermaphroditus, transformed by
nymph Salmacis, 47, 141
Hermes. *See* Mercury
Hephaestus. *See* Vulcan
Herse, loved by Mercury, 127
Herse, Mercury and Aglauros (Poussin),
138
Hersilia, Sabine wife of Romulus,
101
HESIOD, early Greek epic poet,
author of *Theogony* and *Works
and Days*, 22, 26–27
Hippolytus, son of Theseus, renamed
Virbius, 131
Hippomenes, lover of Atalanta, 81
HOFFMAN and LASDUN (editors),

Medusa, mortal Gorgon slain by
Perseus, 90, 108
Meleager, son of Althaea, kills uncles
in hunting quarrel, 93
Memnon, son of Aurora, Ethiopian
prince killed at Troy, 72–73
Mercury, son of Jupiter
kills Argos, 17
punishes informer Battus, woos
Herse, and punishes Aglauros,
123
Midas, king of Phrygia, and Bacchus,
134
Chaucer, Shakespeare, Hawthorne,
144
Duffy, 145
Minerva (also Pallas) punishes
Arachne, 51, 53–55, 111, 126
Minos, son of Jupiter and Europa, 36
Minotaur, monstrous son of Pasiphae
and bull from the sea, 108
Minyeidae (daughters of Minyas),
refuses to worship Bacchus,
turned into bats, 43–48
Mnestra, daughter of Erysichthon,
given power of shapeshifting by
Neptune, 13
Morpheus, dream impersonator, 86
Muses, daughters of Jupiter and
Memory, 51–52. *See also* Calliope
Myrrha, daughter of Cinyras, mother
of Adonis, 6, 75, 78–80, 134, 141

NABOKOV, Vladimir, on the natural
cycle of insect metamorphosis,
140
NAEVIUS, third-century B.C.E epic
poet, his *Punic War*, 6
Narcissus, son of Liriope, beloved by
Echo, died of self-love, 44–46
Neptune, brother of Jupiter, 9, 29
Caenis, 54, 62

causes Achilles' death in revenge for
death of Cycnus, 99
competes with Pallas for patronage
of Athens, 54
rapes Mnestra, 13
Nessus, centaur, 64, 95
Nestor, king of Pylos, his experiences,
32, 63, 98
NICANDER, second-century B.C.E
Alexandrian poet of metamorphoses, 14, 120
Niobe, wife of Amphion, loses all her
children, 69–70
Numa, second king of Rome, 101,
114, 118

Ocyroe, prophetic daughter of
Chiron, 120, 126
Odysseus. *See* Ulysses
Orithyia, daughter of Pandion, raped
by Boreas, 64
Orpheus, son of Apollo and Calliope,
57–58
goes to Hades for Eurydice but loses
her, 57
his program of songs, 76–82
killed by Maenads, 57, 124

PACUVIUS, second-century B.C.E.
Roman tragic poet, 41
Pan, pursues nymph Syrinx, 17
Pandion, king of Athens. *See*
Philomela, Procne, Orithyia
Paris, prince of Troy, kills Achilles, 99
PARTHENIUS, first-century B.C.E.
Greek poet, friend of Virgil and
Gallus, 14
Pegasus, flying horse born of Medusa,
creates Hippocrene, 108
Peirithous, Lapith prince, friend of
Theseus, 92
his wedding, 109

Peleus, husband of Thetis, father of
Achilles; kills brother Phocus,
85–86, 134

Pentheus, king of Thebes, son of
Echion and Agave, 41–43

Periclymenus, shapeshifting brother of
Nestor, 98

Persephone, Ovid's preferred name for
Proserpina, daughter of Ceres, 53

Perseus, son of Jupiter and Danae,
kills Medusa, rescues Andromeda,
90–92
uses Medusa-head to kill his rival
Phineus and other enemies, 92

Phaethon, son of Sol and Clymene;
fatal chariot ride, 18, 31–34, 141

Philemon. *See* Baucis

Philomela, sister of Procne, daughter of
King Pandion of Athens; raped by
Tereus, 55, 65–66
Shakespeare, 142–43
Hollander, Hughes, 146–48

Picus, Italian prince, lover of Canens,
transformed by Circe, 11–12

Pierides, daughters of Pieros, compete
with muses, 52

PIERO DI COSIMO, sixteenth-
century Florentine painter, 134–35

Polydorus, son of Priam and Hecuba,
murdered by Thracian king Polymestor, 71–72

Polyxena, daughter of Priam and
Hecuba, sacrificed to shade of
Achilles, 71–72

Pomona (nymph), beloved by Vertumnus, 149

POUSSIN, NICOLAS, French
seventeenth-century painter,
137–39

Procne, daughter of Pandion of
Athens, wife of Tereus, mother
of Itys, 55, 65–66, 105

Procris, wife of Cephalus, 83–85
death painted by Piero di Cosimo,
134

Prometheus, benefactor and in some
traditions maker of mankind, 25

Proteus, prophetic old man of the sea,
12–13, 32

Pygmalion, sculptor rewarded by
Venus when his statue of ideal
woman becomes his wife, 26,
59–60 (grandfather of Cinyras,
great-grandfather of Myrrha)

Pyramus, lover of Thisbe, 46

Pyrrha, daughter of Epimetheus;
cousin and wife of Deucalion,
30

Pythagoras, Greek sixth-century
philosopher, taught in southern
Italy, 47, 114–18

Quirinus, divine identity of deified
Romulus, 101

QUINTILIAN, first-century C.E.
Roman teacher and critic, 119

RAPHAEL, Italian sixteenth-century
painter, 129

RILKE, Rainer Maria, 133

Romulus, twin son of Mars and Ilia,
founder and first king of Rome,
15, 100–101

Rumor (Fama), 112–13

Salmacis (nymph), transforms Hermaphroditus, 47

Scylla, daughter of king Nisus of
Megara, 75
nymph loved by Glaucus, turned
into sea-monster by Circe, 9, 10,
106, 128

Semele, daughter of Cadmus, mother
of Bacchus, 39–40

SENECA (The Younger)
    Natural Questions, 116, 140
    tragedy *Thyestes*, 143
SHAKESPEARE
    Midsummer Night's Dream, 143
    Titus Andronicus, 142–43
    Winter's Tale, 143–44
Silenus, half human associate of
    Bacchus, 16–17 (Virgil *Ecl.* 6)
Sol (Sun God), father of Phaethon,
    31–34
    informs on adultery of Mars and
    Venus, rapes Leucothoe, 46–47
SOPHOCLES, fifth-century B.C.E.
    Athenian tragic poet
    Niobe, 70–71
    Tereus, 65
STATIUS, first-century C.E. Latin
    poet, 140
Stoics, Hellenistic and Roman philo-
    sophical school, 22, 23

Teiresias, Theban prophet, changes to
    and from female sex, 40
    warns Pentheus, 41
Tereus, king of Thrace, marries
    Procne, rapes her sister
    Philomela, 65–66
Themis, goddess of justice, first patron
    of oracle at Delphi, 29
THEOCRITUS, third-century B.C.E.
    Hellenistic pastoral poet, 120, 129
Theseus, son of Aegeus king of
    Athens, 92
    takes part in boar hunt, 93, 127

Thetis, wife of Peleus and mother of
    Achilles, 13, 86
Tisiphone, a Fury, 48, 111
TITIAN, sixteenth-century Venetian
    painter, 135–38
Triton, 29, 39
Turnus, 91, 99

Ulysses (Odysseus), 8–10, 99. *See also*
    s.v. Homer, *Odyssey*

VARRO OF ATAX, author of Latin
    Argonautica, 74
Venus, wife of Vulcan, 59
    adultery with Mars, 46
    her love of Adonis, 78
    requests deification for Aeneas,
    100
    requests deification for Caesar,
    102
Vertumnus, shapeshifting nature god,
    lover of Pomona, 149
VIRGIL, Ovid's immediate pred-
    ecessor, Augustan epic poet,
    constantly emulated or "cor-
    rected" in *Metamorphoses*
    Aeneid, 3, 5, 6, 9, 26
    Eclogues: *Ecl.* 2, 130; *Ecl.* 6, 14, 22,
    52, 121
    Georgics, 13, 57
    Orpheus in Hades, 115, 117, 124
    Rumor (*Fama*), 114–30
    shield of Aeneas, 48, 94, 99, 102,
    111, 113
Vulcan, husband of Venus, 46

General Index

Adultery
  Jupiter, 16
  Venus and Mars, 46
Ages of man, golden age, 27
Art
  the artist as creator, 58, 59
  in competition with Nature, 25–26
Athens, 54, 65, 92, 117

Boasting, 15, 38, 53, 70, 128, 129

Centaurs, 63, 98, 109–10, 116
Childbirth, 67, 80
  Bacchus' incubation by Jupiter,
    39
Cities
  opposed to country, wilderness, 38,
    41, 46
  rise and fall of, 117–18
Comedy, 125–26, 130
Commemoration by festivals
  Adonia, 82
  Hyacinthia, 78
  by wedding gift of amber, 34

Contests
  in fertility, 68
  in music and verse, 52, 56
  between Neptune and Athene for
    patronage of Athens, 54
  in tapestry, 53–55
Cosmic creator as craftsman, 21
  as molder of clay statuettes, 25

Deification
  Aeneas, 99–100
  future deification of Augustus, 103
  Hercules, 97
  Julius Caesar, 102–3
  Romulus, 100–101
Dreams, 86
  Morpheus and other dream special-
    ists, 112
Drugs, 8, 9,10, 48

Egypt/Egyptians, 31, 52–53, 94, 102
  animal deities, 53
  Isis, 62
  in Odyssey, 13